YOU ARE WHAT YOU DON'T SAY

Finding a New Paradigm for Business Communication

DAVID DAY

D.L. Day

You Are What You Don't Say:
Finding a New Paradigm for Business Communication
David Day

Paperback Edition - © Copyright 2016
ISBN - 9780692654491

Hardback Edition © Copyright 2023 by David Day
ISBN - 979-8-9871396-3-9

Tenth Anniversary Revision - This update is a Tenth Anniversary version that has been edited and expanded to account for new developments in business in the 2020s. (*Any citation should mention this version to be accurate in the page reference.)*

Permissions: ddayauthor@gmail.com

This book is dedicated to Jeannette McGinnis and the beauty of her incredible life (1916-2023)

— and —

to Ronald Gossling for his kind approach to life and business

Introduction

> Tell them what you're going to tell them. Tell them, then tell them what you told them.

Too many people believe that's all they need to know about business communication. Unfortunately, the well-worn approach might just guarantee one could say something no one understands three times instead of just once. Repetition could bring reinforcement, but it doesn't necessarily create understanding nor persuasion. The maxim is also the kind of oversimplification that doesn't work well in an era when technology amplifies and parses every nuance of our interactions.

There is little doubt that the way the world conducts business is in upheaval. Changes in technology, wealth patterns, diversity, geographical distribution of work, and in many other areas are driving a need for new approaches to business communication.

Longer lifespans and health improvements have also brought a circumstance in which there may be three or four generations communicating at work together. We humans have had a difficult time evolving our societal and psychological reactions at the same rate technology has driven change. As this book is now being revised in 2026, the explosive growth of Artificial Intelligence has overwhelmed many of our expectations about business information.

Our new world of business interaction has become a strange mix of old and new, appropriate and inappropriate, effective and ineffective, and can include too many downright disrespectful and failed attempts at dialogue. Even with all of the enormous changes in technology, the way people work and interact and the overwhelming demands placed on humans' ability to rapidly exchange information, there has been almost no societal adaptation of guidelines for effective communication.

This is not a little book about where to put your hands when you talk. The world needs much more than that. Business in the twenty-first century is moving and changing so rapidly that success can only come to individuals and organizations who are fluid, innovative and creative in their approaches and their exchange of information.

THIS BOOK:

- Brings an understanding of the status quo in business communication
- Examines where that status quo falls short and the consequences
- Finds lessons learned in how business communication got to where it is today
- Explores the desirable elements of a better communication paradigm
- Seeks to help calibrate a communication moral compass for our technological age

- Provides compelling incentive to improve communication
- Gives practical steps toward enhancing innovation, creativity, credibility and success through better communication
- Gives some insight into the introduction of Artificial Intelligence into the workplace and what that may mean to communication

Lots of specific business examples are included here to relate the information to real-world business experience. Those looking for a book of pithy sayings like "tell them what you told them," with six bullet points, a moving story and a model will find much more than that here. The examination undertaken will address motivation and human interactions that go beyond just the spoken dialogue in business.

This writing is designed for readers who want to understand why certain things work in communicating and how some communication approaches are far better than others in today's business environment.

PART I

A look at how society and business communicate now

ONE

A Disturbing Status Quo

As modern humans, we are all inundated with information. We live surrounded by a cacophony of voices. Increasingly, individuals and organizations are in search of a platform on which they can opine. Our society is inundated by media promotions. We are pelted with canned audio instructions. We've become the subject of endless research to determine which message will come closest to home for us, with the goal of moving us to some action. We can no longer tell what is "real" and what is computer-generated.

Even if it's just to proclaim our thoughts in 146 characters at a time, we flock to social media in an effort to be heard amid the chatter. We have developed a culture in which we are convinced that the more aggressively, more dramatically, more frequently messages are proclaimed, the more true, believable and effective they will be. We are pounded by a depressing media that feeds on conflict, hate, anger, hostility and destruction.

The affairs of our modern society are increasingly dividing us into political, ethnic, philosophical and socio-economic entrenchments. These divisions limit the scope of our meaningful conversations at work and with friends. Many of us, under the influence of this society, spend hours watching media programs that are driven by the need to shock, frighten, or anger us. We narrow the scope of our dialogue by huddling in increasingly narrow philosophy-centric groups. In many cases, this is done for us by media analytics that decide what herd we should be rustled into today and habe studied very effective means to make that happen.

The major networks fill news shows with designated and paid opinion mongers who are carefully selected to fire up a good argument. They position those paid guests as representing the opinions of society in general, even when the opinions are terribly biased, self-serving, or contrived to create drama.

In the United States, it is increasingly difficult to find international news because the media sources are so busy formulating audience-building drama about the domestic issues that divide or entice us.

The political rhetoric has sharpened to the point that one spokesman for a political think tank could recently suggest publicly that the President of the United States should be "hung, drawn and quartered," and no one seemed to be too terribly shocked by the comment.

Incivility is seen as having reached epidemic proportions in the United States. It is creating divisiveness and rancor, and politicians and the media are fueling it. A 2014 poll of U.S. adults over eighteen years old revealed that:

> Nearly all Americans, 95 percent, say civility is a problem, with three-quarters (74 percent) saying civility has declined in the past few years and two-thirds (67 percent) saying it is a major problem today. Seventy percent also say that incivility in this country has risen to "crisis" levels, up from 65 percent in 2014.

> Asked to identify the groups contributing most to the lack of civility in society, both likely voters and the overall public cite politicians, the Internet/social media and the news media as the top three sources — each being named by more than half the respondents.[1]

When we arrive at corporate or public venues, we bring with us the divisions that have been fired by the commercialization of violence, fear, anger and conflict.

Entertainment is so fed by violence that viewers' stress response is invoked repeatedly, even in the midst of an evening of television, video games, or movies. A recent check of the listings for a major cable programming provider during midsummer (when there were no school nights) showed that of twenty-five listed as "Top Movies," fourteen contained scenes of marked violence. More disturbing still are the instances where violence is so over-the-top that it actually becomes comedy, and we laugh.

One would hope that we could all find safety at home, but the violence isn't just in the media. The US Centers for Disease Control and Prevention has reported that the cost to society of Intimate Partner Violence (IPV) just toward women in the United States exceeds 5.8 billion dollars per year. And each day, we all take our over-exercised stress response and our emotional baggage to work with us.

Corporate business models have migrated toward those in which dehumanization, expendability and abuse are the marks of climbing the corporate ladder and "playing with the big dogs" at the top of the income heap. We attend endless meetings where we are "heard," but only in the context of a flood of jargon-filled, technically clandestine, corporate lingo.

Opinions in such meetings are mostly limited to those who have the power to give them. These are frequently rendered in a state too isolated from reality to be relevant. Too frequently, employees are subjected to meetings attended by people with such poor preparation that they become simply a pooling of ignorance, and the only benefit is getting people out of their cubicle for an hour. Often, these meetings become a showcase for insecure corporate climbers who fear they may go unnoticed if they don't apply overbearing fanfare.

Too many in business meetings barely tolerate that others are speaking, more invested in what they have to say in response than in the complete thought that triggered the response. I have also been in online meetings where forty people spent four hours watching two arrogant executives discuss a single issue while the forty were not asked to contribute even a single comment.

Little wonder some people are so determined to finally be heard when they get home, they are willing to post everything but their most intimate bodily functions (and sometimes those) on social media. This is presumable in hopes that someone, somewhere will care that they are right now having an omelet or enjoying a new pillow.

A Business Perspective

In over thirty years of business consulting and research, I have looked for the modern challenges and solutions for effective communication. I've watched enormously successful companies and leaders and carefully considered what distinguishes them from the mundane. I've seen companies and individuals fail in internal and external communication because of detachment and arrogance.

This book is based on those years of observation and will explore where we as a society now find ourselves in communicating in our personal and corporate interactions, how we got here and how to find a better paradigm.

Whether on a corporate or personal level, there are

powerful patterns that define the communication parameters for success. There are striking similarities between what is needed for corporate and for personal communication to succeed.

Much is being made right now of "Leadership Development." People I know in the Leadership business say, "Being a good communicator comes from being a good leader." My friends in the Communication business say, "Being a good leader comes from being a good communicator." Whatever the characterization of the evolution, whether one will be a failure, a follower, a manager, or a leader usually hinges on the choice of the approaches taken in the tone of interactions with others.

These approaches are now colored, bastardized, assisted, cheapened, or damned by the increasing incursion of the use of AI augmentation of those interactions.

The nature and importance of such choices have migrated dramatically in our high-tech world. Society is at a crossroads in establishing new expectations and definitions of how humans should communicate.

Not only are there decisions to be made by society, but some extremely important personal decisions each individual has to make in how to approach the current communication environment. These personal choices could profoundly and immediately have an impact on an individual's success, popularity, happiness and even health.

Upcoming chapters are designed to clearly walk the reader through the nature, objectives and consequences of those important communication choices. The goal is to help recognize some quite tangible positive, or negative, impacts you may be having on yourself, colleagues and those you love.

> "And, above all, may silence make you strong." – Chief Dan George[2]

TWO

Successfully Mean?

Of course, business communication is multifaceted. There is no question that there are times when the willingness to be confrontational and even tough is an important factor of leadership. To celebrate and reward meanness, however, is a sure way to undermine what should be the ultimate goals of good business communication. The environment we enter in 2026 is one in which mean confrontation has been shockingly elevated in the national discourse in the United States.

How Mean Do You Have to be to Succeed?

Generally, no two business people would have the same answer to that question. Most will agree that business success sometimes takes some demonstration of a hard edge. A rather popular current school of thought suggests that being nice in business is a luxury. More recent, on the other hand, is an attitude that twenty-first-century competitive business demands such innovative thinking from each member of an entire team that respectful consideration and affirmation are a critical part of leadership.

Modern humans occupy a hard world made to seem even more threatening by a constant barrage of stories of conflict, death, war, insanity and absurdity in the media. The internet, video games, television, news magazines, movies, and our own personal conversations can be full of images that depict mean, hostile activities and outcomes.

Now, explosive conflict lunges at some in highly realistic super high definition, seventy-five-inch television. Previous generations simply didn't have planted in their subconscious high definition images of a flock of pterodactyls swooping down to pluck people off the street.

Clearly, the boundaries between the individual's conscious mind (that can sort out fact from fiction) and subconscious mind (that is always on the lookout for personal threat) are frequently breached with images of confrontation and hostility. Because of that frequent challenge to get the stress response in tune with reality, modern humans stay on edge.

It's not known at this point how much constant exposure to words of conflict, controversy and downright nastiness has impacted the business and personal interactions in society. What is known is that there has been a trend toward marginalizing the place of the individual in the social and corporate world and a move toward sacrificing civility and respect.

Marketing strategists are trying to gather as much information on all of us as possible so we can be sorted into bins of income, or politics, general interest, sexual proclivities, spending, education and more. Then we receive various forms of data designed to reinforce, dissuade, or somehow capitalize on our characteristics, so our inclinations are always being tuned, exploited, or assaulted. We are always being fired up in some respects.

In order to understand how we as techno-humans got to our current condition in corporate and personal communicating, it's important to look at the evolution of attitudes.

In the workplace in recent years, people have sometimes been told that they are their own version of a brand, a product. They have to come up with and promote their own "branding" as an individual worker. "Decide what your own brand is and be ready and willing to promote that at any time," some are told. In other words, they have to market themselves, be their own advocate and not count on an employer to keep them on board. Mentoring seemed to go out of style, have a comeback, then fade away again.

There is little security in most large corporations when the big cost-cutting knife comes out and downsizing kicks in to pump up the bottom line. Even smaller organizations may be bought out or have management changes that trigger a justifiable feeling of insecurity in their employees. "Every-Person-for-themselves" can become the rule of the day.

Bye Bye American Pie

The procedure for mustering out of a large corporation has become somewhat standard. Even an executive may come to work and find what turns out to be a "goodbye meeting" on their calendar (the company may be scheduling these with hundreds of people in fifteen-minute increments).

At the meeting with their immediate boss and someone from HR, the employees may find that their corporate internet access was cut off the moment the meeting started. They are asked to turn over their keys, phone, badge, etc. A piece of paper is given to explain the severance pay and process. A security guard is called in as an escort. They are given a couple of cardboard boxes so they can clean out their office and exit the building.

It doesn't matter if they have been with the company for fifteen years, know all of the company secrets, have friends up and down the halls or are two years away from retirement. One moment, they are a trusted employee and confidant with access, and in the next, they are someone not to be trusted, to be cut off from any access and accompanied by an armed guard.

One fact that was not taken into account in the early establishment of this procedure in corporations was that *these terminated employees often arrived home with their tears and their cardboard boxes to face their children, who are now the young people dominating the workplace.* Having seen their parents in such a state, young workers may have found reason in those experiences to develop mistrust and caution when dealing with large business organizations. They may be reluctant to fully invest themselves and their trust.

The number of employees in corporations who cause disruption when they are terminated from employment may be even less than one percent, but everyone is treated as a risk and potential criminal. It is the expediency of this approach that drives it. In many cases, the Human Resources people may know exactly who the troublemakers might be, but everyone is treated equally with little respect and with calculated disempowerment to avoid confrontation with the small percentage who might cause trouble.

My friend, the late Barbara Evans, was for many years a therapist in a city where there are lots of big high-tech companies, and she had as her clients many executives who had been through the downsizing experience. "It's real annihilation," she once told me, with a touch of disgust, adding:

> "When the employer has a security guard walk people out with that cardboard box, in many cases, it has taken much more from the terminated employee than their jobs. They walk out at the moment annihilated as a human being, as a professional, as someone with worth and dignity; they are tossed away with a very destructive ceremony. Some take a

> long time to recover, and some, having undergone the purge, never get back all of their sense of security or professionalism, knowing that any minute their income and, to whatever extent, identity can be pulled out from under them."

In many large companies, employees know this process. Whatever sense of security one might develop, there is always the underlying possibility that on any day, within thirty minutes to an hour, you and every vestige of your residency could be set out on the parking lot. We can't be sure of the long-range impacts of this kind of reality. Does it make people work harder? Does it make them insulated from developing allegiances?

This guarded walk to the company gate may sometimes be based more on corporate financial expediency or management jockeying than on merit. Despite that fact, a downsized employee can become tainted with the loss, carry a stigma of diminished self-esteem, and have a scarred employment record for years. In a society of feigned meritocracy, one can be left rather bewildered by the experience of being plucked from the flock.

For some executives, implementing layoffs can be one of the most difficult and troubling parts of the job. Others can be quite insulated from the human side of the process.

Just as some medical research scientists have learned to see sometimes troubling adverse side effects of treatment in terms of "thousand patient years" of the mass of people treated, some business leaders stake everything on the bottom line for the greater corporate welfare. At times, layoffs are not even done to enhance the long-term bottom line, but to achieve the bonus attached to reaching a short-sighted quarterly goal. They may even be done to create a meme of corporate frugality for investors.

Despite mass layoffs and job insecurity, the popular perception is that our twenty-first century world operates as a meritocracy. It's a belief that those who are deserving through hard work and competitiveness, brilliance, determination and loyalty will reap the benefits of their merits. The undermining of that concept, while still perpetuating the theory, is a source of a good deal of resentment in today's business world.

The advent of Diversity, Equity and Inclusion (DEI) programs and the subsequent overnight demise and destruction of those have created further mistrust.

Unfortunately, in this environment of insecurity and lost meritocracy, there has developed almost a celebration of meanness in some business circles.

A sub-headline in a June 6, 2014, *Harvard Business Review* blog read, "Recognize That Being Nice Is an Outdated Strategy."[1]

Promoting Psychopaths

Psychologists have done a great deal of research in identifying what they refer to as "The Dark Triad," or three personality traits that are considered antisocial and even dangerous. These are identified as Psychopathy (insensitive and wants to control everything), Machiavellianism (manipulative and believes the end justifies the means), and Narcissism (likes to be praised and get special treatment). All three of these personality types can be abusive and destructive in their efforts to reach their own bent goals.

Ignoring social norms, these persons may be quite aggressive, impulsive, non-empathetic and extremely manipulative in their abuse of whatever power they may gain.[2] Unfortunately, the churning influence of enormous change in our work cultures and circumstances has led to a surge in the promotion of Dark Triad leadership in many corporations.

In their book *Snakes in Suits*, Paul Babiak and Robert Hare tell this story in detail. They speak of the rise in the ranks of people with psychopathic traits because they bring to the confusing state of current business an *appearance* of confidence, strength and calm.[3]

What psychopaths actually bring is an arrogant, detached and narcissistic charade that sacrifices the dignity of everyone who works for them.

Young executives often get the message that they have to be tough to succeed. While this may, to a certain extent, be true, there seems to be no one willing to draw clear lines between what is appropriate business tough and what is just mean. Frequently, being mean is confused with being willing to face conflict and confrontation. Handling challenging interactions is an important part of the job of leadership. Being a jerk isn't.

There has been a lot of writing in business publications recently emphasizing that business leaders have to learn how to confront conflict. Avoiding conflict at whatever cost can be quite harmful both in business and in one's personal life. I have consulted with some large organizations where democracy was taken a little too seriously, and conflict of any kind was frowned upon. In those organizations, indecision, stalemate and endless, fruitless discussion of issues were commonplace. The ability to challenge and confront with respect and an appropriate tone is an important mark of a good leader. Meanness isn't.

About twenty years ago, companies were beginning to challenge the hierarchical model for conducting business. There began to be more emphasis on networking and team dynamics in the workplace. Unfortunately, the movement toward short-term shareholder benefit goals and big incentive bonuses for higher-level and mid-level executives sacrificed some of the gains made in that regard.

Lots of business books had argued that the de-emphasis of the hierarchy could result in greater productivity. It is strange that, in the name of productivity, the pyramid structure for management returned to such power as it has. The resentment resulting from such a shift back toward command and control and income differential is marked in many of today's workplaces and has fed into the rise of the Dark Triad in management ranks.

Just as children in a family system respond best to an appropriate level of structure and discipline, an organization works best when there is appropriate structure and discipline, and there are reasonable expectations. Teams that have a dynamic level of openness, creativity, discussion and co-authorship function best when there are leaders who are willing to end the discussion when needed, make the final decisions, and take responsibility for the consequences.

When, however, there is hierarchy for reasons other than order and efficiency, there are increased challenges in communication. When there is hierarchy without responsibility, and it is posing as distributed leadership, it is a recipe for disaster.

When so much money is at stake in relation to the position one holds, no individual on a business team may want to be stuck with blame. Certainly, no ownership can be expected of others where no ownership is taken by leadership. Unfortunately, a destructive corporate environment of refusing to take ownership can be one of the outcomes of the creation of a faux meritocracy and of mean leadership.

WHEN IT GETS PERSONAL

Some bosses are just mean. Character Jim Arbus in the movie *Horrible Bosses* said it this way: "...and it would have been the perfect job, if not for one evil, crazy bitch..."[4]

According to a 2014 study commissioned by the Workplace Bullying Institute (WBI), 27% of Americans have experienced abusive conduct at work.[5]

Isn't it ironic that in a time when civilized laws have been passed to prevent discrimination and harassment, bullying has become an epidemic?

The fact is that there is a distinction between legally defined aggressive actions against a protected class of individuals and the bullying of everybody equally.

BullyingStatistics.org points out that one of the differentiators is whether a boss is simply indiscriminately abusive of everyone. That person may be a bad manager, but unless a few individuals are being unjustifiably singled out it may not be bullying.[6]

Strangely, there may be safety in just being mean all around. One must consider, however, the possible big picture consequences. According to the United States Department of Labor in a census conducted as recently as 2012, workplace homicide was the third most prevalent cause of death on the job for Americans and a top-ranking cause of death (second only to transportation accidents) for women in the workplace.[7] The Department of Labor Statistics for 2014 showed 404 workplace homicides (an average of more than one a day).[8] This may be one of the explanations for the guarded walk to the gate for terminated employees. There appear to be no statistics showing how many homicides were carried out by employees who had lost their jobs, versus those who were just angry while they were still employed.

It would be nice to be able to say very clearly that meanness of bosses and fellow employees is immediately bad for business. It would help to be able to show that abused employees become non-cooperative and hostile, and the overall productivity goes down, but this may not always be the case.

It is certainly not a new idea that abused persons will sometimes work to cater to the approval of their abusers. They may believe they enhance their track up the corporate ladder by cowering to the bullying. The added stress of economic downturn or general employment competition can make this more pronounced.

This phenomenon may explain why some organizations have rampant meanness that doesn't seem to cut productivity. The acceptance of the bullying of fellow employees may be connected in part to the inevitable employee reviews that may determine the order of any downsizing.

One might ask, then, if in some organizations periodic layoffs are cost-cutting or a part of an elaborate negative motivational scheme to keep a workforce under control. Frankly, they can also be part of blatant stock or management drama and meme creation intended to impress stock analysts. By whatever degree the company engages in this short-sighted, obvious manipulation, it can expect to have that soon become transparent to the employees, with inevitable loss of trust and engagement.

A segment of the corporate world often supports a mean corporate culture with a mistaken idea that there are productivity benefits, and that the risks of being too nice to employees can be unacceptable. Ultimately, the benefits are questionable, and there are enormous social and financial risks that have evolved from our migration toward mean.

Frequently mean doesn't go all the way to the top. Maybe it's just a symptom of climbing the corporate ladder that meanness becomes not quite so necessary when one gets to the top. Many higher-level executives are cordial, gregarious and invested in interacting with others. In over thirty years of consulting with top executives, I have only run into a small number of Presidents or CEOs who were just generally mean.

One was so disruptive and harsh in his criticism of his people that an entire team, gathered with him in a hotel preparing for a regulatory meeting, hid from him for an entire day so they could quietly resolve issues and solve problems. Weeks later, a TV stock market commentator called this guy by name and told him that, for the company to succeed, he needed to get out of the way and let his employees do their job.

In another session, a CEO dressed down his company's top executive in front of a group of about a dozen professional experts. "You are pitiful," he told the wealthy, highly-educated executive, "you are giving idiotic, sniveling, incoherent answers, you stupid *f__k*." It was one of those moments when all of the air goes out of the room, and everyone just sits quietly stunned. In this case, there was so much money at stake for every person in the room that no one dared challenge the cruelty.

The rudeness did, however, work just the opposite of what must have been the perpetrator's goals. Not only did the abused team member get worse and more hesitant in his communicating, but everyone in the room had the creativity, energy and brilliance sucked out of their interactions and ability to prepare for the pending important conference.

Sometimes, even at the highest levels in companies, executives are called to be accountable for their meanness.

We know of a meeting of top officers for a large high-tech firm in which the CEO, exasperated with reports of abuse, finally said to the company President, "Let's face it, if ten thousand people say you're an asshole, you're probably an asshole." In a short time, that President was no longer with the company.

All workplace abuse is not overt. It's common to talk about the "Inner Circle" of the corporate leaders of a company. What is less discussed is that down the chain, at lower levels of the organization, this inner circle phenomenon replicates. Managers often have their allies knitted in a tight group around them. The result can be that other employees find themselves on the outside and being ignored or taken for granted. Such clandestine groupings can be quite abusive in their own way.

In *Mobbing: Emotional Abuse in the American Workplace,* Noa Davenport, Ruth Distler and Gail Pursell Elliot present the results of two decades of research on the phenomenon of employees being group bullied or subjected to "mobbing" at work. They chronicle the way in which workplace bullies band together to isolate, intimidate and discredit individuals and may even force them out of an organization.[9]

It doesn't take overt verbal abuse for someone on the job (or in some other type of group) to experience that their self-image and feeling of worth are under attack. Proximity, body language and exclusion can be powerful communicators. This type of abuse is certainly most likely to surface in an organization where advancement is based more on office politics and misrepresentations of productivity rather than legitimate merit.

As problematic as bullying may be, a study at the Sauder School of Business at the University of British Columbia suggests that ignoring persons at the workplace might actually be more damaging than overt abuse. The study, entitled *Is Negative Attention Better Than No Attention? The Comparative Effects of Ostracism and Harassment At Work* presented evidence that ostracizing someone may create more damage than bullying.

"We've been taught that ignoring someone is socially preferable–if you don't have something nice to say, don't say anything at all," says Sauder Professor Sandra Robinson, who co-authored the study. "But ostracism actually leads people to feel more helpless, like they're not worthy of any attention at all."[10]

For a leader in an organization, the personal and organizational challenge becomes a matter of striking a strategic balance between alliances and aristocracies, assertiveness and meanness, appropriate control and chaotic openness. Like tap dancing on a greased bowling ball, it takes constant attention, that is, unless one can find some fundamental principles that guide the interactions.

We will focus much of our discussion at the business level, but you will see later in the book that the same challenges and principles can apply to interpersonal communication with the world around us. There can be no healthy and productive dialogue in an environment where meanness thrives.

In my work with executives, I have found apprehension that in the current environment, kindness can be misinterpreted as weakness, and deferring to others' opinions might be seen as a lack of decisiveness. We will show in this book that respectful, human, humane, appropriately-balanced interaction is the best mark of strength and of respected, decisive leadership.

PART II

How we got here in communicating, and the consequence of our approach

THREE

Are We Keepers?

> Then the Lord said to Cain, "Where is Abel your brother?"
>
> He said, "I do not know. Am I my brother's keeper?"
>
> And He said, "What have you done? The voice of your brother's blood cries out to me from the ground." – Genesis 4:9-10 (KJV)

How did some businesses get so mean, and what has it done to the corporate psyche? Do we reject or embrace the open invitation to meanness that is obvious in today's public discourse?

Two very interesting concepts are at work now in business. One is the idea that a corporation is a person. The other is the recent embrace of "Objectivism." The philosophy, popularized by author Ayn Rand, suggests the moral objective of a person should be to satisfy *individual* needs and achieve one's own happiness.

> My philosophy, in essence, is the concept of man as a heroic being, with his own happiness as the moral purpose of his life, with productive achievement as his noblest activity, and reason as his only absolute. – Ayn Rand, *Atlas Shrugged* [1]

A newly popularized movement has been to bring these two concepts, the corporation as a person and Objectivism, together. How can a corporation be "happy" as Rand suggests is necessary for successful personhood?

We will explore here ways in which the corporate dynamic is now so dysfunctional that the satisfaction of individual needs and, certainly, the "happiness" of corporate personhood is grossly misunderstood and misappropriated.

The earlier chapter addressed meanness in business. This attitude may be the outgrowth of embracing an idea that "corporate" does not refer to the body of participants, employees or even stockholders in an organization. Rather, the corporate personhood is seen as some autonomous entity with its own identity and even its own religion.

This concept suggests that meanness can be an inherent part of happiness in corporate personhood. That is certainly hard to address because consciousness of a corporation doesn't exist, or one could convert GE to Buddhism. In order to do that, the changes would have to take place among live people and their consciousness within the corporation.

In some circumstances, the goals of corporate personhood are misinterpreted by the highest-placed executives to mean simply the satisfaction of the ambitions and fortunes of a very small handful of people at the top. (This, unfortunately, has been carried over by some into the highest levels of government and perceptions of what government should be.)

The Corporation as a Happy Person

It would be easy to make the argument that to be happy, the corporate personhood should strive for the happiness of its parts. A living person certainly finds it hard to find happiness when various body parts are sick or malfunctioning. If, then, we are to discuss happiness in corporate personhood, we are led to discuss corporate health.

Objectivism is unable to handle the interdependence of beings. This is one of the reasons the debate over Global Climate Change has brought such passion. It demonstrates the enormous impact of interdependency that is inclusive of the giant corporate "persons" of the world and the smallest and weakest living creatures on the planet.

In order to pursue Objectivism, one has to discount the fact that there are body parts and that they can produce pleasure, pain, empowerment or disability. We will show here ways in which sickness in a corporate environment makes for a sick corporate communication and a sick corporate personhood. This sickness in a societal environment creates a sick communication and culture with no capacity to thrive.

Unfortunately, we can't just declare a corporation "sick" or incompetent and have it committed. All we can do when a corporation is running amok and out of control is to somehow redirect, correct, or constrain its parts. The same is true of a society. Any thought of a societal personhood must acknowledge that its parts are real people.

Increasingly, employees are sensing a disempowerment that puts more space between them and the corporate personhood. A study by the National Institute of Occupational Safety and Health (NIOSH) of the US declared:

> Research is needed to better understand how new work systems affect workers' capacity to influence job conditions and opportunities for learning and growth, and in turn, the impact on safety and health in the workplace. Increased worker control and learning opportunities are recognized in the job stress literature as powerful antidotes to stress and illness. But concern exists that various worker participatory or involvement strategies may often be more ceremonial than

> substantive, having little meaningful influence on worker empowerment—or perhaps even eroding workers' means to influence job conditions through more traditional labor-management mechanisms such as collective bargaining.[2]

Whether related to a growing feeling of disempowerment or identified specifically in relationship to a philosophy, an attitude of self-focused, isolated harshness is growing in our interactions.

Much of recent business, political, and personal philosophy has promoted the idea that there is some great competitive, even hateful, divide between a popularized objectivism and an equally dramatized altruism. This conflict has become a polarizing political game. People are taking sides on these philosophical differences, whether they realize it or not. Some factions may decry "big business greed" on the one side, "Socialist do-gooders" on the other, but what is at issue here is the conflict of basic philosophies, Altruism versus Objectivism. Is it "all for one," "one for all," or "free for all?"

What Does This Have to do With Communication?

It's important to discuss corporate philosophy in a book about communication because this philosophical conflict has a great deal to do with how people misunderstand each other in business and in society in general. Given the great conflict inherent in work/life balance, corporations are driving unreal expectations of production and heavily impacting our perceptions of who we are as humans and the responsibility we have to each other. This phenomenon is being exacerbated by the introduction of AI to our lives and the ambiguity it brings to the future of work and work relationships.

Altruism is seen as a "Regard for others, both natural and

moral, without regard for oneself."[3] In some respects, conservative politics would brand any government or corporate manifestation of the philosophy "Socialism."

For a corporate personhood to be altruistic, it would have to put the welfare of others before its own welfare. One must decide whether customers are what one would consider "others," employees, "others," stockholders, "others." Are the top corporate executives "others?" Or, are "others" everyone but the top executives?

How far from the core of the organization does one have to search to define stakeholders who are "others?" One can certainly make an argument that corporations cannot be altruistic because the corporate personhood must continue to exist and be heavily devoted to its own survival and needs. But what parts define this personhood?

We can also find similar complications in embracing Objectivism to the benefit of self. In the case of individual or corporate personhood, just how autonomous is this "self" we seek to preserve? Most corporations can't continue to exist without meeting the needs of somebody.

We would argue that the world is so interdependent, so interconnected, that neither Objectivism nor Altruism can successfully dominate. In fact, throughout history, there is evidence that, except for occasional examples of extraordinary greed or selfless heroism, neither pure objectivism nor altruism can long survive in a civilized society. Let's point out that "civilized" may be a very important term here.

Let's suggest that it would be fraudulent to claim one can apply either pure Objectivism or pure Altruism to business, because neither can succeed on a standalone basis as the operational philosophy of "corporate person" in our complicated world. Competitive language around such an application to societal structures is also damaging and paralyzing.

Modern-day pundits frequently position adherence to the

principles of Objectivism against the practice of Altruism, with the idea that there can't be a functional middle ground. There can, has been for centuries and should be in the future for society to function properly.

There may be bonuses and rewards that feed expediency for highest level executives to embrace individual Objectivism to the detriment of the health of the various parts of the body of the corporate "person." We can, however, use the example of the living person to say that when all of the blood rushes to the head, the body eventually passes out. Even from the beginning of time, "my brother's keeper" is a fundamental reality of human existence.

If, as NIOSH hints in its publication on work changes, workers are increasingly feeling disempowered, a part of the body of a corporate personhood is becoming detached and disinterested. This has prompted a popular meme of "Employee Engagement" in business publications and discussions.

Inequality, excessive and hostile ladder climbing, runaway greed, faltering customer service and general communicated meanness in the workplace are symptoms of our current sickness in the corporate personhood.

In the words of Genesis, "What have you done?"

FOUR

Complicated Track to Communication Trouble

In the past four decades, the paradigm for corporate communication has undergone a dramatic and random change. In many ways, society has drifted in an uncontrolled way in communication philosophies, methods and tools. There are also important aspects of interactions we as a society should have altered in response to the enormous changes in the business environment, but we haven't.

Having previously discussed where we now find ourselves in our personal, societal and corporate experience, it's helpful to suggest a better paradigm. To do that, it is important to examine what came unraveled in business interactions and how it happened. How did we get here?

An earlier chapter quoted a National Institute of Occupational Safety and Health statement that: "Organizational practices have changed dramatically in the new economy." What an understatement! Since 1983, modern humans have literally reinvented ourselves. US Patent Office statistics [1] show that between 1983 and 2013 patent applications for inventions increased by about 500%, as compared to only about a 25% increase in the previous three decades.

We, as a modern society, have undergone enormous changes brought on, only in part, by the explosion of technological innovation. A psychologist might suggest that if a living person were to undergo as much change as our corporate personhoods have undergone in a relatively short period, they would probably get sick or die.

In just three decades the gender, age and ethnic makeup of the work force, the kind of work that is done, attitudes toward employees and employment, the geographic locations for the work being done, the tools for work, the office environment, compensation structure, the scope of the markets, our marketing approach, attitudes about retirement and many of our business philosophies have all changed. Even within many individual business categories, there has been huge and persistent change.

Consider the electric utility business as an example. Shortly after the invention of the light bulb, there was a concerted push to wire the cities. Soon, the government became involved in electrifying the countryside and bringing lighting to farms and rural communities. The increased need brought a driving demand for the creation of more and more electric generation technology.

Technicians who had for years settled into jobs with coal, fuel oil and hydro generation then had to make way for nuclear engineers. This was followed by a period of intense involvement of state utility commissions that set about to regulate the industry.

Next was a phase when utility companies were looking for all kinds of businesses where they could stash their money outside the electric utility. They bought everything from communication companies to hotels and got into areas they sometimes didn't understand, with often disastrous results.

Strangely, companies then faced *deregulation* by some utility commissions and encouragement for competition and market-driven businesses. Deregulation was followed quickly by partial or full *re-regulation* in most states where deregulation didn't work so well. Now, along came environmental concerns and billions of dollars in retrofitting plants to meet new standards. On the heels of these concerns, the industry had to bring solar, wind and increased emphasis on natural gas, and even the reintroduction of the idea of building new nuclear plants into the mix. This remix of generation meant building a vast new grid of transmission lines to bring the new energy resources to market.

Now, suddenly, everyone is experiencing thousands of attempts to hack into their control systems, and the industry is having to spend billions on security upgrades. Imagine spending the past thirty years as a leader in the electric utility industry. It has been a wild ride for anybody associated with that business and one that takes more fluidity than many sane people can tolerate.

Next, there emerged an unraveling of federal environmental regulation and a hostility to wind and solar power that gave a backhand to decades of utility company planning and priorities. The President of the United States, speaking at an economic forum in Switzerland announced that "only stupid people" invest in wind energy.

Surprisingly and suddenly, solar and wind fell from grace in the federal political scene, and those programs went begging. This happened on the cusp of the development of huge batteries that allowed these facilities to store energy and provide it to the grid in peak demand periods (thus increasing their value to a system tremendously). It has been a bit of a circus and a crazy ride for those onboard.

Now, as in many industries, electric utilities are dealing with integration of AI into their business. This is encroaching fast in technical, operational and regulatory functions.

We can also consider the sweeping changes in the pharmaceutical field. Constant evolution of knowledge and application has brought about an entirely new era of therapies and approaches.

When I was a child, doctors were housed in "Medical Arts Buildings." The "art" of medicine still exists, but increasingly it is enhanced by statistical measurements of experience and by scientific developments in the ability to manipulate and tune the human system. From the earliest uses of pharmacological chemistry to a growing understanding of the body of responses on a cellular level, the business is in a constant state of change.

Now, treatments can include harvesting an individual's own cells, enhancing their ability to fight disease and returning them to the patient more powerfully equipped to achieve a cure. The approach can now be on a DNA and molecular level. A dramatic shift in both the approach to medicine and the expertise it takes to implement it. It is a dramatic shift also in the makeup of the staffing and in the communication in the business.

With all of the technological changes, migration toward more and more reliance on statistical data as evidence of efficacy and safety became the norm.

In the midst of this in 2025, came an administration in Washington that dramatically shifted the focus of the Food and Drug Administration, challenged the use of vaccines, questioned the scientific analytic methods for approving drugs and stripped the FDA of decades of experience and expertise. This is paired with a new and ambiguously described paradigm for how pharmaceutical approvals should proceed.

Also with pharma, Artificial Intelligence is changing things dramatically. From the search for new drugs, to finding new uses for old ones and throughout the operational business, AI is having an impact with dramatic changes.

The electric utility and pharmaceutical industries are cited here as just a couple of examples of the incredible movement in technology, demand, politics and approaches to business that have challenged our human interaction in many types of businesses.

Most work now involves much more complicated technology. Many jobs shift frequently in the types and details of new information teams have to digest. In the midst of the exponential technology growth of the past thirty years, businesses have specifically:

- Added many more women and minorities to the workforce
- Moved workers temporarily and permanently around the globe as never before
- Changed in many ways what they produce and how they produce
- Begun a shift toward heavy use of Artificial Intelligence
- Created cubicles and at-home work environments
- Engaged many more salaried and contracted workers versus hourly workers
- Changed the expectations for hours worked
- Used international outsourcing more heavily
- Hardened security, openness and access
- Changed previously held views of customer service
- Added Artificial Intelligence to many aspects of business and work with, as yet, eventual implications

...and the list goes on.

In the middle of all of this change, we are using many if the same old verbal and written communication rules and tools.

Whose Stakes Are They?

Even greater impact on business communication has been generated by a sea-change in corporate philosophy. A few years ago, management writings began to reflect that executives were emphasizing what one could call "Shareholder value." That is the idea that the interest of the stockholders and stock price, even in short-term gains, were the highest priority in running a company.

This was favored over stakeholder value, which would take into consideration all of the impact on all of the stakeholders in the success and continued growth of a company. A problem arose because executive bonuses became linked solidly to increases in quick profitability and stock price increases.

While debate has raged about the preferability of shareholder value versus stakeholder value, neither is ultimately good for business when it is misused to the detriment of the other. Simply stated, when the body parts and long-term health of the corporate person are compromised for short-term gain and enrichment of a few executives at the top, the company eventually suffers.

Confused employees are constantly having to shift their approach to work and their corporate dialogue to keep up with this changing dynamic. The language of driving, short-term gain, seldom takes into account the long term impacts of stress and disincentives in the ranks.

A Misplaced Value Creates a Mess

Unfortunately, shareholder value is a broad term that was, in the past three decades, wildly left open to some very dangerous interpretation. Were these fluid increases in stock price of value to the corporate person? If so, at what time point and for how long? Did these spikes in stock price bring the added value of long-term stability and growth? For some companies, almost never.

Corporations are now discovering that an extended period of misappropriation by some executives for the cause of short-term bonuses, disguised as bringing stakeholder value created a mud pit of complications.

Wall Street strategist Michael J. Mauboussin asserts that the idea of seeing shareholder value as maximizing the short-term stock price and doing whatever it takes to engineer an ever-higher market price is a "profound misunderstanding." He says, "The premise of shareholder value, properly understood, is that if a company builds value, the stock price will eventually follow."[2]

A profound misunderstanding of what constituted shareholder value drove some unhealthy decision-making in the past decade, and the damage will take years to repair.

Let's look, for example, at an idea that shareholder value had to be measured by quarterly results. One can provide lots of dollars to incentivize the executives to deliver those results. With a new societal emphasis on loyalty to self, employees often developed a laser focus on bonuses. There are lots of manipulation points in an organization that can be shuffled to change short-range outcomes.

In fact, moving money around to meet financial goals became a rather popular accounting trick in the 90s. It was engaging in a similar "revenue smoothing" that revealed an even deeper problem at a major computer manufacturer in 2007.

In what was seen as one of the more blatant examples of revenue manipulation at the time, the Securities and Exchange Commission (SEC) reported settling with Dell, Inc. for a penalty of $100 million based on an allegation Dell used fraudulent accounting to make it falsely appear that the company was consistently meeting Wall Street earnings targets and reducing its operating expenses. SEC charged that this was done to cover for payments Dell was getting from Intel to avoid using Advanced Micro Devices products. Financial goals were being met, bonuses were flowing, stock prices were climbing, but (according to the SEC) things were not as they seemed.[3]

Since that time Dell has taken definitive steps to make sure the company has a culture such that it won't find itself in that kind of spot again. The Dell scandal could be seen as an interesting example of shareholder value (or stock value) objectives gone wrong.

As another example, consider that one of the more expeditious, but misguided, methods of maximizing results became employee downsizing. This was done sometimes indiscriminately to send a message to financial analysts and temporarily drive up the stock price. Older workers were a good target because they could be lured into early retirement.

The claim of improvement in temporary shareholder value misrepresented the fact that cutting those older employees was sacrificing an enormous amount of expertise, experience and corporate memory that was impossible to evaluate in dollars.

Loss of corporate memory and experience are not things that impact a company this quarter, but their loss may have an impact on productivity and efficiency for years to come.

That has, in fact, been the case in hundreds of organizations, including our public schools, where good teaching knowledge has taken a back seat to technological prowess.

Rather than bringing long-term experienced teachers up to speed with on-the-job training in utilizing new technology, schools are throwing them out along with their incredible experience and insight into how to impart knowledge to kids, while at the same time turning schools into a big business.

Going Nuclear

How about one more example? Over twenty years ago, the nuclear industry gradually began to whittle at its mature workforce. Highly trained, experienced and educated workers were encouraged to take their "brand" elsewhere as they aged. Many of them, in aggravation, took it to the golf course. Now nuclear facilities must still be maintained and nuclear power is newly appreciated, but the world will soon face a near-crisis in staffing nuclear science fields with mature, experienced nuclear operators.

A survey by the Oak Ridge Institute for Science and Education has reported that Nuclear Engineering Bachelor's Degrees earned in the US between 2021 and 2023 occurred at a rate lower than levels reported from 2016 – 2019 by nearly 27%. The number of bachelor's degrees awarded in 2022 was significantly below the levels reported in the previous decade.[4]

In an article entitled "Shortage of Young Engineers Threatens Nuclear Renaissance." the *Wall Street Journal* quoted Energy Department data showing that the U.S the nuclear engineer field currently stands at about 68,000 people.

The article quoted Department of Energy data as suggesting this number would need to grow to more than 200,000 to meet its forecasts that see nuclear power tripling by 2050.[5]

This projected growth presumably includes the introduction of new types of smaller nuclear facilities, as well as the coming wave of energy through nuclear fusion technology, expected to begin in the 2030s.

In a move signaling a new attitude toward nuclear operations, the U.S. Department of Energy's Hanford site in Washington announced the revival of a nuclear facility that has been closed for about 30 years. The Fuel and Materials Examination

Facility (FMEF) will reopen and be revamped as a production and testing center for advanced nuclear fuel.

This comes at a time when there is thought of new nuclear construction and many existing nuclear fission plants may operate for another thirty years. They will then need to be dismantled by experts who have experience in what they're doing. Where is the shareholder value in the loss of experience when expert staffing becomes sparse or non-existent?

One would think students would be rushing to nuclear engineering schools. The fact is that the transition to the future is further complicated by the fact that existing nuclear plants may no longer be price-competitive.

Of the 99 nuclear reactors in the United States, some 36 have shut down since 1997.[6]

Numerous sources attribute the looming potential for closure of such plants to increased unplanned outages and increasing maintenance costs, as well as the fact that so many may be nearing the end of (or far beyond) their design lifespan.

Of course, there is no way of separating the attribution of cause for escalating costs from the implications of the loss of profound corporate knowledge with the exit of so many nuclear engineers and technicians over time.

Any corporation that looked only for driving the most imminent quarterly results and bonuses was kicking a risky and expensive can down the road.

Now, when there exists an opportunity to revive and reinvigorate nuclear energy, we are searching around for knowledge and staffing in an environment that is daunting.

Perhaps, AI will fill in some of these gaps, but that transition is complicated and presents challenges of its own.

Over the course of this long nuclear journey, communication experts who knew that boosting public trust is building one of the vital assets of corporate growth and stability had their work cut out for them. The rush to capitalize on cost-cutting for short-term gains prevailed for some time. In many cases, consulting came to focus on crisis response when long-hidden corporate sins were ultimately exposed.

The Road to More Problems

In some businesses, crises have been brought on because delays were made on maintenance, or training, or updating technology because of a desire to meet short-term cost-saving targets and distribute bonuses.

In some companies, a long-term crisis was assured because the system encouraged promotion to the highest leadership positions of persons who were locked into a reactive stage of adult development in which one only reacts to evolving conditions, rather than searching for creative and considered approaches for longer-range outcomes.

This approach to living requires more energy and yields less productivity than higher states of personal maturity. It's also a stage that ultimately generates a workplace fear dialogue that is harmful to long-term corporate health.

While the period of misplaced shareholder value abuse is not wholly responsible for the disruption of corporate culture and faulty communication and relationships, it clearly made a significant contribution to a long period of loss of employee commitment.

Not only did external communication suffer in this environment, but many employees also locked themselves down in their willingness to be transparent in communication with management. If bad news is not suffered well at the top, the cover-ups can start with the person mopping the floor. Corporate climbers can distort reality to whatever extent they have the ear of the decision maker.

There should be a good measure of trepidation in a high-placed corporate executive who discovers that only good news gets to the top. It's quite true, however, that when an organization encourages suppression of authenticity and personal integrity, the communication flow to the top shuts down.

This experience of suppression of interaction comes with an assurance that employees who have reached a higher and dramatically more productive stage of adult development will probably leave. This occurs because exploration, innovation and creativity can't flourish in an oppressive communication environment focused only on bonuses.

Corporate Culture in a Petri Dish

As a consultant frequently called upon to deal with crises, I can say that many can be traced to problems with corporate culture. An endemic, near-fatal flaw in corporate culture can evolve over a short time in a deceptive, good news only environment. Emphasis on short-term, bonus-driven goals can foster such a culture.

Once it's in place, such a damaged culture is extremely challenging and can become a quite expensive, time-consuming and traumatic problem to repair. Unless an organization has a candid culture profile undertaken and is willing to come to terms with individual leadership misdirection, repair may be impossible.

Like a dysfunctional family, organizations can be defined by their leadership and by the reactionary response of the individual parts. Unfortunately, many organizations so afflicted don't fix the underlying problem, but simply move from one crisis to the next. Like a dysfunctional family, they perpetuate the "family lie" that there are no problems at the top. Sadly, almost twenty years of misplaced Objectivism and a misdirected concept of shareholder value have created a lot of organizations that are so afflicted.

It's important to point out that, although the term "corporate culture" is used here, corporations don't have a culture. The culture is generated by individuals in that corporation, and the tone is set from the top. This environment is a derivative of the moral compass held by leadership.

One could question whether it was corporate culture or misguided individual action that led to problems for a major international bank. BNP Paribas (BNPP) describes itself as a leading bank in the Eurozone and a major global bank. In 2012, they had revenues of about 38.8 billion euros. They promote themselves as "The Bank for a Changing World."

According to a June 2014 news release from the New York State Department of Financial Services, "BNPP engaged in a long-standing scheme that illegally funneled money to countries involved in terrorism and genocide." The department charged that "BNPP, with knowledge of multiple senior executives, set about on a contrived effort to conceal their more than $190 Billion in transactions for clients subject to U.S. sanctions, including Sudan, Iran and Cuba."

The allegations charge that the COO "signed off on continuing illicit transactions at a meeting where he asked minutes not to be taken." The DFS quoted a communication from the North American Head of Ethics/Compliance for BNPP as saying: "The dirty little secret isn't so secret anymore, *oui*?"[7]

Governor Andrew M. Cuomo announced a New York State Department of Financial Services (DFS) enforcement action related to violations of law and significant misconduct at BNPP. A DFS statement said that:

> BNPP's violations were particularly egregious in part because they continued for many years after other banks were sanctioned for similar violations; involved numerous schemes expressly designed to deceive regulators; and were committed with the knowledge of multiple senior executives.[8]

What was the cost of all of this? BNPP was ordered to pay 8.9 billion dollars to federal and state authorities, terminate senior executives, and suspend US dollar clearing operations for one year at the business lines where the misconduct was alleged to have been centered. Persons terminated or separated from the bank included the CEO, Executive Committee Advisor, and former Head of Compliance, Group Head of Debt Capital Markets, Group Head of Structured Finance for the Corporate Investment Bank, and the Head of Ethics and Compliance for North America. Forty-five additional employees were disciplined.

The company issued a press release announcing a major overhaul of the BNP Paribas internal control system. In response to the reorganization, BNP Paribas Group CEO Jean-Laurent Bonnafé is quoted as saying: "As a leader in the European banking industry, we must aim to be exemplary in our conduct."[9]

With 185,000 employees and about 4.8 billion euros in net income, can one chalk the problems up to corporate culture, or merely suggest that in that huge company, there was a set of ethics held by certain individuals that seemed to justify specific extenuating circumstances under which it's okay to break rules?

Did the procedural changes exterminate any ethics bug that may have brought on the crisis? Was it a matter of corporate culture, or the acts of a group of individuals who may have now been purged from the company?

A lesson to be learned is how a management ethics judgment can be communicated through an organization with enormous implications. It's something to consider carefully the next time someone mentions "corporate culture." The language, emphasis and communication approach to expectations can have an enormous impact on the idea of what is considered acceptable in an organization. The "culture" will reflect in the communication in ways that can often make even hidden faults transparent.

Is it Getting Better?

There are hints that the tide has shifted, and the climate of recognizing stakeholder value as the only goal of corporate culture is taking hold. Former Labor Secretary Robert Reich in an article entitled "Rebirth of Stakeholder Capitalism," put it this way:

> We may be witnessing the beginning of a return to a form of capitalism that was taken for granted in America sixty years ago. Then, most CEOs assumed they were responsible for all their stakeholders.[10]

Many states have authorized companies to incorporate into what are called "Benefit Corporations." These companies have to declare a mission and charter to operate in a way that benefits society, employees and stakeholders, including shareholders. Lest one think all corporations are so inclined, apparently, these states assume that's not the case.

It's the integrity of the individuals in an organization that forms the corporate culture. It is the ethics of individuals that form the integrity of a corporation. It's the ability to communicate those ethics in day-to-day interactions that makes them stick.

Losing Our Corporate Memory

One of the changes that impacted (especially the tech) industry was the quick rise of new, quite technically savvy, high-paid, young executives with very little leadership training or experience. They also, in many cases, knew nothing at all about managing or interacting effectively with people who were working under stress.

Unfortunately, many needed a lot of work done to improve their social and emotional intelligence, but it didn't happen. That development was coupled with the workplace attitudes discussed in previous chapters and the departure of mature mentors, and resulted in a great deal of miscommunication, misunderstanding, overreaction and immature decision making.

Suddenly, there was a high demand for executive coaches to fix leadership problems. In many cases, those coaches discovered and reported to businesses that leadership was heavily loaded with folks who had not reached higher stages of adult development. High intelligence for technology didn't necessarily equal high emotional intelligence.

Lost somewhere in all of this evolution was the concept of civility and deliberate intent in what needed to be communicated. This included when, to whom, why and in what way.

Contemporary with the corporate philosophy changes we have described, society has undergone a sweeping shift in focus, growing out of the technology revolution.

Technology has driven the economy, education, politics and values. The world has experienced an unprecedented popularity of purely engineering/technical think. Creativity became limited mostly to developing hardware. The technology revolution created an environment in which we as consumers, can suddenly be confronted with an assumption by high-tech designers that we all want to wear our computers on our faces.

Rather than, as the old adage says, "necessity is the mother of invention," invention has become the mother of necessity. The engineering/technology world has developed things because it could, then set about to sell consumers on the idea of why everyone will need those things.

In this rapidly-changing kingdom of technology, people could be run through an organization with great rapidity and little concern for civility in interactions. Some who saw technological proposals and asked, "but why would we need that?" were soon on the other side of the door. The era has become a good example of corporate personhood ignoring potential sickness in its body parts.

Technology, the Great Vacuum

In this invention-is-the-mother-of-necessity mode, there was created an incredible global vehicle for communicating on the web, and it happened before anyone decided to ask, "What content is going to go into that vehicle, and how should industry qualify folks to develop that content?" The result has become a social media with billions of pictures of kids, cats, dogs and sex parts. There is a residing confusion as to how it should all make sense.

While it is only fair to say that there has been an enormous explosion in access to information of all kinds, it's also true that much of that information seems to be migrating toward a form that is a quick read, distilled, simplified and of questionable validity. Much of the content simply conforms to a consumer need for expediency and often departs from any standards of journalism, art, verification, intellectualism and good taste. Too often, it is analytics of the most base viewer interest driving the content.

Popularized now on social media sites is the shorthand term "TLDR." This "Too Long Didn't Read" epitomizes an idea that the mere length of a communication disqualifies it from valid consideration.

There are few signs that a need for meaningful content will be filled anytime soon. Society has cut funding for the arts in schools and attacked the concept of Liberal Arts education.

Talk show hosts have been heard laughing at the idea that anyone would want a degree in Art, Philosophy, or History. Sadly, the potential for intellectual endeavor that should be fueling public creativity and content in this new global connection is becoming extinct.

In some major universities, students can get an Engineering degree with as few as six hours of history and three hours of some elective in Liberal Arts. Twenty-first-century society has focused on education strictly for employment. In fact, the world is now seeing the phenomenon of the "nano degree" as offered by Udacity, an online education company that brings an even tighter focus to matching a finely tuned curriculum to a specific job area.

This new form of university may be quite important for our continued productivity. As the nature of our work changes, this education just for jobs may well be seen as exactly what is needed to staff business organizations. In remarks in 2012, United States Secretary of Labor Hilda L. Solis predicted:

> Over the next decade, nearly half of all job openings nationwide will be for "middle-skill" jobs. These are positions that require more than a high school diploma, but less than a four-year college degree. These are white-collar, blue-collar and green-collar jobs that pay family-sustaining wages. Actually, they're more than just jobs. They're pathways to better-paying careers.[11]

The concept of half of all jobs requiring less than a college diploma is a concession to the idea that education is strictly to fulfill requirements for getting a job. It ignores the need for emotional, social and intellectual intelligence required for effective interaction, skills often learned in college. If high schools and junior colleges were imparting these abilities to students, it would be a big step in improving communication in the world. Unfortunately, Emotional Intelligence is not high on the curriculum of most schools today.

In a great reshuffle that is swiftly bearing down on us, a definition of what are AI/robotic jobs, and what are human jobs, will completely redefine our human education requirements.

Some college students are flocking to schools of communication, primarily in response to a dream they will be stars of some kind in the mass media. Many want to focus on how to say things, rather than what to say, or learning how to search for what should be said. Communication professor friends of mine tell me many freshmen come to university with minimal skills in critical thinking and little appreciation for the intellectual exploration that is so necessary for good journalism or creative communication.

Some also come indoctrinated with the idea that open-minded, critical thinking is somehow sinister. If such students don't change before they become communication thought leaders in business organizations, society may be in for a strange anti-intellectual revolution.

Reactive and closed-minded corporate communication could become the norm for generations. Unfortunate also is the increasing political pressure on professors and educational institutions not to teach or encourage critical thinking.

From these various channels of preparation, the peopling of work and society has begun to produce segments ill-prepared to deal with the enormous consequences of choosing direction for our various outlets, organizations, endeavors and interactions.

This new population addition that is so addicted to quick digital texting may also emerge with little appreciation for societal and interpersonal face-to-face communication fundamentals that must be adhered to in a civilized world. The public is sometimes left with little to talk about except the output of the media circus.

Sadly, some of the business and social world have not embraced a new understanding of the adaptations needed in our communication to keep our interactions civil, clear, respectful and sensitive to long-range impacts in a changing world.

There is, instead, a sociopolitical migration toward name-calling, cruelty, denial, blatant prevarication and tricky and deceptive framing of issues.

To help develop a better communication paradigm, the next few chapters present some specific concepts and directions that can set society on a better course toward filling the void created by meaningless content. Although one can't suddenly create a markedly improved societal intellect, it is possible to attempt to inspire important thinking.

A desirable goal is to improve understanding of how to communicate appropriately in this complicated world. A more ambitious goal also undertaken here is to inspire in some small way an understanding of what is needed to make certain the vast and growing capabilities of society's technical reach are filled with some level of communicative content designed to improve the human condition and lift the human spirit.

~

FIVE

Meanness and Consequences

> Dialogue is the elixir of life and chronic loneliness its lethal poison. – James J. Lynch

Maybe, as individuals, we can't afford to be so mean and detached. Abrupt and harsh approaches to communicating may be creating much more damage than we realize by leaving us quite unprepared for our immediate future.

Work has undergone a big paradigm shift over the past few decades. In a publication, *The Changing Organization of Work and the Safety and Health of Working People,* the National Institute of Occupational Safety and Health of the United States acknowledged the world is in rather uncharted territory:

> Organizational practices have changed dramatically in the new economy. To compete more effectively, many companies have restructured themselves and downsized their workforces, increased their reliance on nontraditional employment practices that depend on temporary workers and contractor-supplied labor, and adopted more flexible and lean production technologies.

> Fears have been raised that these trends are resulting in a variety of potentially stressful or hazardous circumstances, such as reduced job stability and increased workload demands. Data suggest, for example, that working time has increased dramatically in the last two decades for prime-age working couples and that workers in the United States now log more hours on the job than their counterparts in most other countries.[1]

Objectivist thinking has created a stronger self-serving, individual survival model of employee participation, with increasing feelings of isolation and ostracism.

The NIOSH publication acknowledges that "...the revolutionary changes occurring in today's workplace have far outpaced our understanding of their implications for work life quality and safety and health on the job."[2]

Science has shown there is transformative power in our words as well as our actions. Passionate words actually change people's brains. Whether negative or positive, they can change the brain structure over time to alter how individuals see reality. Now, there is scientific evidence that we as humans absolutely see the world differently when someone loves us.

The perception of reality is also altered when people are subjected to high stress and a disrespectful, hateful environment. Human brains change, and the perception of reality is revised.

In a very real way, the stresses, hostility and isolation generated by workplace and home environments are changing the very make-up of the human brain, killing people and therefore dealing a blow to the health of the personhood of corporations and the corporate society.

The National Institute for Occupational Safety and Health (NIOSH) gives this warning:

> ...effects of job stress on chronic diseases are more difficult to see because chronic diseases take a long time to develop and can be influenced by many factors other than stress. Nonetheless, evidence is rapidly accumulating to suggest that stress plays an important role in several types of chronic health problems, especially cardiovascular disease, musculoskeletal disorders and psychological disorders.[3]

There is a mounting and convincing store of evidence that stress is unraveling all of us and our society in a slow-moving, but unimpeded epidemic.

Stress is clearly making workers sick. According to the Centers for Disease Control and Prevention:

> Short-lived or infrequent episodes of stress pose little risk. But when stressful situations go unresolved, the body is kept in a constant state of activation, which increases the rate of wear and tear to biological systems. Ultimately, fatigue or damage results and the ability of the body to repair and defend itself can become seriously compromised. As a result, the risk of injury or disease escalates.[4]

James J. Lynch in *A Cry Unheard New Insights Into the Medical Consequences of Loneliness* cites scientific evidence from a large number of studies that document the health and mortality impacts of the meanness, stress and isolation generated by cold and detached interactions in today's business. He suggests humans' cardiovascular systems can be exhausted by repeated triggering of the fight or flight mechanism of emotional arousal that is not accompanied by the strenuous physical manifestations of fighting or running away.[5]

Based on recent health trends, it is growing ever more apparent that New Age cultural forces that disturb, disrupt and destroy human dialogue must be viewed with the same concern and alarm as has been brought to bear on other plagues, infectious diseases, viruses, bacteria and cancers.[6]

The medical impacts of the pressures people place on each other are staggering. Although it is very difficult to sort out exact statistics that associate the relationship between meanness, hostility, isolation and circulatory diseases, there is a great deal of scientific evidence of a strong association. The big picture on heart disease is not a good one. The summary health statistics for U.S. adults *in the National Health Interview Survey, 2012* told this story:

> Overall, 11% of adults aged 18 and over had ever been told by a doctor or other health professional that they had heart disease, 6% had ever been told they had coronary heart disease, 24% had been told on two or more visits that they had hypertension and 3% had ever been told they had a stroke.[7]

That is about 75.5 million people with hypertension and 34.5 million people who have been diagnosed as having heart disease.

Then there are the troubling outcomes having to do with sadness and psychological distress:

> Overall, 10% of adults felt sad, 6% felt hopeless, 5% felt worthless and 13% felt that everything is an effort for all, most, or some of the time during the 30 days prior to the interview. ...16% of adults had feelings of nervousness, and 16% of adults had feelings of restlessness for all, most, or some of the time during the 30 days prior to the interview. Three percent of adults experienced serious psychological distress during the 30 days prior to the interview.[8]

Recent studies suggest stress is associated with inflammatory response and can be an outgrowth of depression, with resultant promotion of inflammatory diseases such as arthritis.[9]

Although there are different kinds of stresses and people may have difficulty identifying as individuals their exact stresses and predicted responses, it's known that a stress response goes quickly from the brain to the body.

When someone confronts danger more quickly than their conscious senses can detect, the amygdala, a contributor to emotional processing in the brain, sends out a distress signal. In a cascade of responses, the body is prompted to release epinephrine (adrenaline), corticotropin-releasing hormone (CRH), adrenocorticotropic hormone and cortisol.

The response includes increased cholesterol in the blood, increased glucose availability, increased energy use, increased fat deposition, insulin resistance and metabolic syndrome. There can also be eventual immune suppression and susceptibility to some infectious diseases, as well as anxiety, depression and reproductive abnormalities.[10]

One can imagine the continuous impact of repeated release of these hormones, fats and blood sugar when there is no real fight or flight, and one is sitting at the desk, stressing over an e-mail or phone call. The result can be long-term disability.

A study at Concordia University in Quebec found there was a dramatic increase in doctor visits for persons in high-stress jobs, versus lower-stress jobs:

> Estimates for the whole population show that high or medium job strain has a positive and statistically significant association with the number of visits to both a general practitioner (GP) and a specialist (SP). On average, the number of GP visits is up to 26% more (IRR = 1.26, 95% CI = 1.19-1.31) for individuals with high strain jobs compared to those in the low job strain category. Similarly, SP visits are up to

> 27% more (IRR = 1.27, 95% CI = 1.14-142) for the high strain category.[11]

Of course, much of the stress can simply be associated with circumstances, but there is also growing evidence that an unquantified portion of the stress we are all experiencing is attributable to our communication methods, language, philosophies and attitudes toward each other.

Changing these habits will bring greater long-term efficiency and success. Even if reducing one's own and others' stress doesn't seem to be a robust business goal, one can't ignore evidence that reducing job stress increases productivity and improves profits. This, of course, may not be by next quarter or in time for the bonus. For those thinking on a larger scale, with longer-range goals, data suggests reducing stress is the only thing that makes sense.

If only for this reason, organizational leadership, including boards of directors, should be intent on identifying, discouraging and changing toxic dialogue.

~

PART III
Fundamental steps toward a better communication paradigm

SIX

Learning From Two Very Different People

The next few chapters explore suggestions for a better communication paradigm in professional and personal lives. By looking at the communication approaches of two individuals, the reader may gain a wealth of insight into some very important communication principles.

Just these two stories could make an observant person contemplate what could be a life-changing self-evaluation. The comparison is offered here to set the stage and to put an understanding in place for a full discussion of communication goals.

This chapter will introduce the reader to two people who communicate differently, with quite different results. One seeks to find identity through what he says. The other is revered and defined more by her willingness to not always speak. In many ways, she is what she doesn't say. It's probably safe to suggest that, at the time of the observation, neither knew the technical specifics of their own communication style.

When I first met Jeannette, she was getting ready to celebrate her eighty-fifth birthday. Jeannette would stand out in any crowd as one of the more gregarious, happy, pleasant people there. Even as she was approaching 90, she had lots of friends, she was very engaged, she traveled a lot within her area of the world, she made friends easily and was always ready to have a day or evening out. She was more amused than impeded by her age.

Jeannette always laughed a lot. Fond of visiting with people, she had been popular as a high school teacher, then moved on to be a college professor. Even when she was surrounded by exciting, young, energetic, brilliant students, she was able to generate laughter and fascination in her audience. Jeannette has traveled the world. She taught in several foreign countries at a time when women just didn't do that sort of thing.

Just before her death at 107, she was far different from most people who might be sitting at home or in a nursing facility, quietly isolated from the world. She never seemed to want to slow down and remained independent, capable and self-directing well into her hundreds. "I'll tell you why I love to shop at Neiman Marcus," she once said. "They don't ask my son what kind of shoes I want. They look at me, and they talk to me."

Sometimes you meet people who just seem special. At first, it was hard to understand or explain, but as soon as I met her, it was clear Jeannette was one of these people. There was something about her personality that was attractive, interesting and stimulating.

For her ninetieth birthday, Jeannette's friends, family and ex-students held a dinner honoring her. About a hundred people were there. From sheriffs to doctors, to attorneys and other professors, people stood to tell stories of how this woman had transformed their lives.

She had secretly checked out library books for high school football players so their buddies wouldn't make fun of them for reading. She had used influence to get people into colleges, even arranging for one girl's lodging with one of her own relatives during a freshman year.

"People tell me I look so good for ninety," Jeannette told the crowd celebrating her birthday. "I say, 'how in the world would you know, you've never seen anybody who was ninety."'

One of the stories she has told in conversation was about traveling with her friends by car in Mexico just a few months before her ninetieth birthday. She was in the company of three younger women friends, all in their eighties. The eighty-two-year-old woman driving was speeding when she was stopped by the Mexican *Policía*.

"Hang your head down, "She said to Jeannette as the officer approached the window. "This woman is ninety years old," she told the officer in Spanish. "We have to get her to a town so we can get her some food and water to take her pills." The officer smiled politely, told them good day, and waved them on. As soon as he was gone, the women burst into guffaws and went back to the business of getting to Monterey.

Over the years, Jeannette became my informal, one-person study in Communication. How could she captivate, entertain and become so endearing in her interactions with people? One of the fortunate enhancements of my life has been that she became my phone buddy. Whenever we can both find the time, we talk about life in general and about our lives in particular.

What I have discovered is that Jeannette, after over sixty years of teaching school, became an expert in kindhearted, loving interrogation. She is a master of assertive listening. "So, David, tell me what's happening in your life," she begins many conversations. That is followed by a stream of jovial, sincere, invested questions that have me excited to tell the latest stories of me.

To each, she will respond with laughter or consolation, a brief, knowing comment, or a supporting silence that encourages me on. Rarely does one of my stories cause her to say, "... that reminds me of when I..."

Finally, I have realized that not until I ask "What about you? What's going on in your life?" do I start to find out about her. Over the years, there have been hours of these conversations. Usually, they find their way back to questions about me or my opinion of something. Little wonder that I just adore her. Who wouldn't?

Her one-hundredth birthday found Jeannette still as invested, curious, masterful, witty and energetic as ever, and the conversations continued. After ten years on the phone, I have learned to also be a sounding board for her. She has taught me how to use active listening as a means to embrace and endear others. She has enriched my life enormously with what she has shared from the richness of hers.

There should be no surprise that I came to love her and find in her conversation an affirmation of the value of my personhood. I came to cherish the idea of that voice of affirmation always being just a phone call away.

In a world where few know how to powerfully listen, I found a diamond mine, a priceless treasure of someone who would invest intelligence, time, energy and a masterful talent in listening to me. A big added bonus is that she has taught me something about how to listen to others and myself.

When asked what has made her such a good communicator, Jeannette traces it back to childhood:

> I grew up with six brothers. If I wanted to have anybody to talk to and not be ignored, I had to find out what interested them. One of my brothers, who was very quiet sometimes, was interested in baseball and history. I found out that if I learned about baseball and history, we could have extended conversations just about any time. Eventually, he would ask about me. Someone once asked me why that brother talked

so little. 'You just haven't found what he wants to talk about,' I told them.

A suggestion that one have an extended phone conversation with a centenarian may, for many people, bring on stereotypes and pre-judgments. Some might expect to hear ramblings and disjointed stories about aches and pains. That is a world apart from the experience of a conversation with Jeannette.

Having read scores of books on communication, I can say that they all struggle to capture the fundamentals of healthy interaction used so expertly by my friend Jeannette. She demonstrates extraordinary communication skills based not only on the experience of growing up with six brothers, but also the life lessons of over five decades of teaching school.

After years of counseling executives of many of the most powerful companies in the world, I can say that the important keys to respect, success and influence can be found in the way Jeannette communicates.

Now a Different Story

I met Jess (not his real name) in a college classroom. In his early twenties, bright, assertive, intelligent, Jess seemed to have the perfect attributes for personal and business success.

He was convincing and brilliant in classroom presentations and responses. It would be easy to predict he would zip through the course with little problem. I first visited with Jess when he stopped me in the hallway to introduce himself and say that he had been impressed by one of my comments in class. Jess was outgoing, engaging and seemed confident. In just a few minutes, I learned a lot about him.

Jess was thrilled to be in school, enjoyed it enormously, was taking fifteen hours and studied and worked most of the time. I knew where he grew up, how many were in his family, that he had excelled in debate. In a ten-minute conversation, he asked not one question.

Over the next semester, there were many similar conversations with Jess. I also watched him interact in the class and in the hallway with other students.

There was a fascinating pattern of communication. Every interjection he made in a discussion seemed intended to somehow cause others to hold him in higher esteem. He told stories that generally involved some way in which he had excelled, or entertained, or succeeded, or heroically struggled. He interrupted others frequently to make his own point. When someone did manage to tell a story or make a comment, Jess seemed to have a competitive ("I can go one better than that") story or declaration.

I also noticed that not a lot of people hung out with Jess. On one occasion, he talked to me about a disappointing job interview when he didn't get the job. Jess said he had "carefully researched" the company that was hiring. (He looked it up on the internet.)

He had prepared a number of short speeches that he would make at various points during the interview. He was certain that it would be, he said, "a slam dunk." "I was very forceful in making sure I got these speeches in," he said, "I wanted them to see that I could be a leader."

As our interaction continued, I pushed ahead with a few closed-ended questions and didn't allow him to interrupt.

> "Did you ask any questions about the interviewer?"
>
> "No," he said in a staccato voice.
>
> "Did you ask anything at all about the job?"
>
> "No, I knew about the job. I showed them that."
>
> "Did you ask any good questions based on your knowledge about the company?"

"No," he said, "but I knew about the company, I told them I knew that."

Finally, Jess did something I had never known him to do in almost an entire semester. He asked an open-ended question. "What do you think went wrong?"

Based on previous conversations with friends who are in Human Resources, I knew I had a few answers for him. I had learned from them that one of the important elements of a job interview is authenticity. "I had a woman come in once who was trying to get a promotion in our company," one of my HR friends told me. "She obviously had read on the internet '*Ten Important Questions To Ask In A Job Interview*,' and dutifully and stiffly worked her way through each of them. She didn't get the promotion because it all seemed so fake."

My friends explain that not asking questions may be fine, if at the end one says something like, "Well, I had some questions about the job and the company, but you seemed to address them all in the interview."

Otherwise, it may change the entire tone of the interview to ask questions like:

"What are the opportunities with the company?"

"What do you like most about working here?"

"I saw XYZ about the company, I'm a little curious, can you tell me..."

The underlying goal is to strive to become a human talking to a human. One should want to become a person in the interaction and not just a statistic or face in the crowd.

Most good interviewers will open the door: "Now, do you have any questions for me about the company or the position?" It isn't that not having questions is, in itself, seen as a big strike against you. It's just that having good, informed questions, offered with the right tone and authenticity, can move you into a different category in your communication with this interviewer.

Assuming he was asking me as a communication expert, I tried to summarize what Jess might want to do differently in his next interview. Then I had a question for him.

"So, what do you think went wrong?"

"Oh, I think it was rigged, and they already knew who they wanted," he answered. The semester soon ended, and that was our last conversation.

In the two examples of individuals shown in this chapter one can see demonstrated communication fundamentals that are at work in most of the personal and corporate successes and disasters of our time. The cases demonstrate the dramatic difference between sincere inquiry and self-serving declaration. To get attention, one must pay attention. It is a rule of exchange.

"Is anyone paying attention?" could be the desperate cry of modern society. Unfortunately, too often, the answer is "no." For those who learn how and when to pay attention and when to ask, when to respond or when to listen, there are worlds of opportunity. There is a chance to change directions for more positive personal and business relationships.[1]

SEVEN

Does Anybody Care?

Just Care.

Sounds simple, right? Caring is the first and most important step toward establishing a better personal and corporate communication paradigm, but caring may be disappearing fast.

One would think it should go without saying that communicators should care about others and about what they are doing, but it has gone without saying for too long. Caring is a prerequisite for undertaking an authentic, meaningful dialogue. That means giving a damn about oneself, giving a damn about the other participants in the dialogue, about the subject, about the immediate impacts of the dialogue on the parties involved and about the lasting consequences of the dialogue. It means you have to stay in touch with your humanity.

Modern business people have become very good actors. Acting like we care is a well-practiced and applied art. To actually care means to invest oneself.

Do you care? Is your care well placed? Are you predisposed to care? Are you surrounded by folks who don't care? Some people operate under a misperception that human endeavors are only for isolated, individual benefit. Too many people are faced with a reality of having become so overwhelmed with family and social activities and taking on what used to be two or three people's jobs at work, that caring has become a luxury they think they can't afford.

This attitude of detachment is reflected on the street in the number of salespeople and service representatives refusing to make eye contact in businesses when they talk to all of us as customers. It's easier not to care when they make no real contact. Even though such detached contact is an in-person interaction, it is even less human than a text or an email.

Similar dehumanizing detachment exists in top-floor offices when outcomes are only seen in the context of bonuses or promotions. Just not caring can certainly be a symptom of an every-person-for-themselves-I-just-want-my-check type of environment.

In such an environment, a heart surgeon, for instance, might know more about how to prescribe and code certain procedures for insurance reimbursement than how many patients have died at his or her hand.

In such an environment, the Chief Financial Officer of a public electric utility, asked in a hearing what the average monthly electric bill of the company's customers might be, may say under oath, "I don't know." That's a measure of arrogance and isolation that has too narrow a focus for business and humanity.

Through words and the actions connected with words, humans define our reality. If we are to identify this reality in a productive, healthy, mutually enhancing way, effective communication must be an authentic dialogue. Authentic dialogue must include investment by the parties involved.

The world we have described so far can easily disrupt this dialogue and replace it with a self-focused, disconnected script of bureaucratic or manipulative blather. The reality this creates for individuals is damaging, unhealthy and suppressive of any potential for creativity or innovation.

Given the challenging environment in which we as modern humans all live, why care? Maybe it's a situation in which one might say, "Oh, this sounds great, we should all care. You start." Why should one care, independent of what others around might be doing or expressing?

I know a minister who, prior to performing weddings, requires that a couple undergo a program of couples counseling. He has a very interesting perspective on fidelity in marriage. Saying that too many people in marriages may hinge their own faithfulness on whether the other spouse is faithful, this minister suggests that fidelity and trustworthiness are character traits that should not be dependent on someone else's actions. "To trust begins with being trustworthy," he says.

He explains that when one commits to fidelity, anything done to violate that fidelity is stealing from the relationship. One decides not to be a thief based on his/her own values, not the values of another. "You control you and each spouse generates trust in the other," he says. So far those marriages performed by this officiant have lasted. Commitment must be devoted first to one's own core values.

To many, to care is seen as an individual act born of choosing individual dignity and integrity. Fake caring is self-destructive to some, but maybe not to everyone. For many, to be isolated from the extended consequences of their detachment and arrogance ultimately erodes their self-esteem and dignity and creates a stress that compromises their health. Later in this chapter will be a presentation of evidence that the natural ability to have empathy is not brain-wired the same for everyone.

It should be acknowledged, of course, that there is a difference between a healthy mental detachment that allows one not to get too emotionally hooked in the stresses of circumstance and a selfish, dispassionate refusal to consider the consequences of one's acts or the hurtful impacts on the recipients of thoughtless comments.

Certainly, a nurse in a trauma center has to operate with some level of emotional detachment to carry out the job and not break down. On the other hand, it would be quite inappropriate for that same nurse to take out anger at hospital administration by snapping at a patient, or refusing to report the mold on the bottom of an operating room keypad. To care appropriately, even under pressure, is a fundamental requirement for a civilized society to remain organized and functioning.

In an article in *Harvard Business Review*, Ernest J. Wilson III, Dean and Walter Annenberg Chair in Communication at the University of Southern California's Annenberg School for Communication and Journalism, reported on a study in which representatives of the school interviewed business leaders to find out what attributes executives must have to succeed in today's economy. One of the five they identified as critical was empathy.[1]

How Are You Wired?

It's just generally assumed in current literature on the subject of leadership that good leaders must have an adequate level of empathy. Are our most successful leaders empathetic? Someday, there will be a medical test to tell. Evidence suggests that many might not be equipped for empathy.

Empathy can have a big impact on communication, and we have traditionally assumed it is learned and cultivated in our interactions. Recent research suggests, in fact, that empathy is genetic and doesn't come naturally to everyone. Work by Sarina Rodrigues, assistant professor of psychology at Oregon State University along with UC Berkeley psychology graduate student Laura Saslow, *et al*. presented strong evidence that the human peptide oxytocin, which functions as both a hormone and neurotransmitter, has influences on social and emotional processes throughout the brain and plays a part in the measure of empathy and stress individuals are capable of experiencing and expressing.

In other words, some people may be just genetically predisposed to be more or less empathetic than others because the difference in the configuration of people's receptors for this peptide can make quite a difference in, not only the empathy response but the stress response they experience and express to the world around them. This can certainly impact what is traditionally seen as communication skills involving empathy.

An allele is a designation of part of the DNA coding; it is a form of a gene located at a specific position on a chromosome and is part of the intricate process that passes traits from parent to child. All humans inherit a variation of this gene or "allele" from each parent. The Rodriques/Saslow study looked at three combinations of gene pairing on the oxytocin receptor.

These are referred to as variations, "GG," "AA" and "AG." Persons with two copies of the G allele (GG) were found to be the most empathetic and experience less stress than members of the AA and AG allele groups, who were found to be less capable of experiencing empathy and more likely to experience stress.[2]

Simply put, the data demonstrate that the ability to experience empathy is hard-wired into our chromosomes.

Imagine the implications for understanding our home, societal and work environments if there were widespread acknowledgment and appreciation for this difference. People react in some instances because they are predisposed for feelings and reactions that are different from others. Imagine also the frustrations of persons who are not pre-wired for empathy, who are told how vital having empathy is for leadership.

(Before one jumps to some sexist conclusion about gender and empathy, it should be noted that the research found no pattern of gender differences in the distribution of this characteristic.)

This is all fairly new research and perhaps one could relate the research even more closely to business if one were to take a next step and study the genetic structure of this oxytocin receptor in relation to various positions and responsibilities held in business. But, until such data exists, we can only guess as to whether persons who are more or less genetically predisposed to empathy rise to the top in organizations. What is the distribution of genetic disposition to empathy in Dark Triad individuals?

It would also be informative to test a hypothesis that one or another of the expressions of this receptor plays a part in whether a person is more or less successful in corporate sales. One unfortunate potential outcome of this kind of research would be if employers or HR departments required a genetic code readout on prospective employees.

For the purpose of our discussion of communication, it's important to note that simply saying "*care*," as we did at the beginning of the chapter, is not going to mean the same thing to all people. If, in fact, caring is an important part of dialogue, what is to become of our better communication paradigm for those persons who are wired for less empathy?

We would suggest that it is in a more decisive and deliberate conscious effort that people can find the motivation to care. In the preceding chapter, when we talked about Jeannette being driven to learn to communicate through a need to get her brothers' attention, we noted how she initially feigned an interest in baseball as a means of dialogue.

It's also true that she grew a real interest in the game and a fascination with her brothers' joy in it. She cared for them, she cared for their interests and she loved the dialogue. Sometimes people are motivated to learn to care in various ways. One reason that could be embraced is the acknowledgment that caring improves dialogue and dialogue can improve ultimate success in most endeavors.

We must acknowledge that as different people interact, they may not have empathy at all, or may have variations in their ability to experience caring. Those variations may include:

- Natural predisposed empathy
- Learned empathy that is prompted by observing the outcomes of the empathy of others
- Goal-focused empathy that sees some specific self-benefit brought on by the well-being or success of others
- Empathy that, although not occurring naturally, is motivated by a generalized higher thought acknowledgment of connectedness and interdependency

Whether operating in social situations, at home, or at work, those who are not empathetic as a natural state may find a powerful operational insight in that last point listed above. If caring for oneself registers as important to an individual, it may be quite helpful to frequently be mindful of the concept of interdependency and interconnectedness.

As self-serving as it may sound to more empathetic persons, those who are less empathetic may be able to function better when they more fully understand the experience of the empathetic and account for that in interactions. We know of no research in this regard, but we could hypothesize that if naturally less empathetic individuals were to find a better avenue for their approach to empathy, it could reduce their stress.

If the reader notices some struggle by the author to put all of this into words, it's because we are talking about experience states and haven't developed much of a vocabulary for these newly discovered differences. It's hard for one person who can't experience a feeling or emotion to get a good understanding of the impact of that feeling or emotion on others. Maybe a new awareness of this experience state difference will help develop a new approach to dialogue about empathy.

Not to leave out the individuals who are hard-wired to be more empathetic, we might say that a little learned detachment in business could be an important thing. Consider, for example, the corporate executive at a small company who tells his employees everything because he believes if he were in their place he would always be more secure knowing exactly what the company is doing.

That kind of empathy and openness could, in fact, compromise the company's ability to take risks and make bold steps because it makes the executive too worried about individual employee reactions to everything. The policy could sacrifice the executive's leadership strength.

An "AA" or "AG" person who is wired for less empathy could certainly be drawn to Objectivism. Pure Altruism could be quite a stretch for such an individual. If, however, that person finds some middle ground that acknowledges the impacts of interaction and the ultimate implications for self, he or she may discover more basis for more meaningful dialogue with quite different individuals.

Think for a moment of the implications of our international politic in recognizing this genetic difference in individuals and striving toward a more universal understanding of empathy.

Certainly, a corporate personhood doesn't have gene expressions or oxytocin receptors. (That's one of the problems, isn't it?) If, however, there is a predominant corporate environment that is non-emphatic or one that is excessively altruistic, the organization may lose the important balance necessary for the dialogue that brings efficiency, productivity and success.

It is, in fact, entirely possible that we, as business leaders, will soon find, with further research, that a significant part of the disconnect between various departments in some of our corporate communities is due to an inability for persons with different expressions of this oxytocin receptor to understand and dialogue effectively with each other.

What we understand to be true now is that, whether or not a person is predisposed to empathy, caring for organizational or personal stakeholders is essential to ultimate success at most endeavors.

Unfortunately, too frequently the business world has searched for the quick way out of this challenge and simply attempted to motivate people with money. Theoretically, in that frame of reference, empathy doesn't matter. This approach unravels, however, when shareholders, stakeholders, employees, or social networks begin to realize that empathy and sincerity are missing.

Perhaps "AAs" and "AGs" stopped reading several paragraphs ago, but if you are still with us, it's important to note that you may very well have been misunderstood for a long time because of the sense of detachment with which you have taken on some tasks. Imagine the understanding that could be gained by more widespread knowledge of the basis for human differences in experiencing empathy.

In almost every case, corporate communication crises must be resolved in part with some kind of expression of empathy for the impacted parties. An ability to find our way to that goal before a crisis erupts could certainly help avoid such crises. This better approach begins with dialogue that finds common ground for understanding how empathy and caring are important in our shared goals.

EIGHT

Communicating With Respect

Who do you think you are?

Seriously, who do you think you are?

Are you important? How important are you? In what context are you categorizing that importance? Are there people who are less important than you? On what basis, money, intellect, power, prestige, position, all of the above? How should that importance be displayed in your interactions, dialogue and demeanor?

Would you answer these questions the same today as you would have ten years ago? How about ten years from now?

"Who do you think you are?" is one of the more important questions in business communication and one that is met with some of the greatest presumption. It's a matter that defines one's expectations and has made or broken many careers.

Obviously, in business, it's important to give and to get respect. At the same time, respect is difficult to define. What is it? How do you know when you have it, or give it?

Respect is variously defined as being associated with dignity, with recognition of another's value and with treating others as one would want to be treated. It is associated with a certain decorum, deference. It's associated with honor and appreciation for opinion, allowing for differences, making way for choices and more. In fact, respect may be understood differently by each individual.

Respect is one of those practices that may be best described by looking at examples of when it is missing. If a ninety-year-old great-grandmother walked into a room full of people and a seventeen-year-old male family member tried to slap her on the behind, everyone in the room would immediately recognize that this was not an appropriate showing of respect. Obviously, this is an outlier example, but the point is that there would be all kinds of things wrong with that disrespectful behavior on the part of the teenager.

Consider the same, very vibrant, very alert ninety-year-old woman walking into a department store and the clerk spending a whole conversation asking her questions through the younger adult with her. Suppose the clerk never makes eye contact with the older person and acts as if the older woman can't think for herself. That is an absence of respect, and on an entirely different basis.

Respect and the Big Picture

Now, on a larger scale, let's look at a controversial example. Communication experts frequently find themselves in the position of Monday morning quarterbacking major crises. "If we had only been there to advise," we contemplate, "the situation could have been much different."

Think of the volatile situation in the U.S. on August 9, 2014, when in Ferguson, Missouri, a police officer shot and killed an eighteen-year-old Black youth. Police shootings of African American young people had been in the news around the United States all summer.

At the same time, drug gangs and thugs of all ethnic origins had been arming themselves with increasingly higher firepower weaponry, and police had developed an increased sense of risk. The subsequent result of this particular encounter was an extended period of demonstrations, riots and police response. Now consider the meaning as it was understood by many watching the events on television.

The propriety of the shooting has been a matter of some debate. What is not so controversial is that the immediate aftermath of the incident and the police organization's communication with the community were not well-handled. Many in the public came to believe the youth was shot while he had his hands in the air in surrender, and that the handling of the entire incident showed disrespect for African Americans.

Clearly, the shooting victim may have been disrespectful, maybe even threatening to the police officer. Perhaps that person may have, moments before, been disrespectful in shoving and stealing from a convenience store clerk. That was one level of disrespect. The discontent and rioting were based on an entirely different level of disrespect. It was based on what was interpreted as a disrespect for the dignity and humanity of an entire group of people and perhaps an entire race.

It was not only the actual shooting, but the subsequent handling of the body, the family and witnesses, information about the deceased, and general attitudes toward the community that brought the ire of demonstrators.

The incident raised a lot of emotions on both sides of the shooting controversy. However one may feel about the incident or its outcomes, the story serves as a good example of *perceptions* of respect or the lack thereof. How might things have been different if the public had believed the body of the dead youth had been appropriately respected, covered and placed in an ambulance?

What if his family had been immediately consoled by a

police counselor at the scene? What if the deceased had not been left in the street for over three hours? What if police had withheld disparaging information about the victim until additional information on the shooting was released?

Based on years of communication consulting, I would say the Governor would not have ultimately called in the National Guard. He might have avoided a situation in which the *perception of disrespect* grew to encompass an entire group of people who saw themselves as being represented by the treatment of one young man. Unfortunately, the people in power were thinking it was only a matter of sorting out the truth and dispensing facts as they wished about one shooting. It wasn't. Rather, it was a matter of understanding *the meaning and* the meaning appeared to many as one of racism and disrespect.

The police shooting example demonstrates the far-reaching definitions, observations and outcomes that can be associated with being perceived as disrespectful. Such a perception can have a pronounced impact on personal, business, and political relationships. In many ways, respect is a matter of seeking mutual understanding and a willingness to earn trust.

Loyalty or Engagement, Is There a Difference?

Now we turn to the matter of respect in business. There have been some writings recently saying that company loyalty is dead and will never return. This was after decades of a nice truce between workers and employers that was based on a feeling of mutual respect for the dignity and worth of organizations and individuals. We are in an era when a great deal depends on whether company leadership is seen as self-confident, self-assured, or insufferably arrogant and disrespectful. Will businesses evolve now to the point that company loyalty can be revived?

Earlier chapters addressed the rise of insecurity in corporate jobs. For decades, relationships between employers and employees were considered to be a matter of shared loyalty. Now, many employees view the series of downsizing, outsourcing, doubling up on the duties of individual employees, and growing disparity between executive and employee pay as a sign that company loyalty to the employee has been abandoned.

Recently, the pendulum has shifted, and employers are discovering that many of their workers are always looking for other jobs. Many business owners would like to hit the loyalty reset button, but that seems pretty much impossible. There is some talk of how to regain the loyalty of employees. In the absence of that, companies are seeking to measure and settle for what we now refer to as "employee engagement." If we can't have loyalty, maybe we can prompt *engagement*, but both depend on mutual respect.

Whether one calls it engagement or loyalty, businesses are building now on a different kind of basis for respect. There remains the individual need for human dignity and deference that has to drive business interactions. A need for personal, respectful interactions has been made more important by the fact that teams now spend so much time communicating via email and text.

It's hard to measure the implications of this factor in terms of what is sacrificed in the loss of the non-verbal exchanges and constant testing of the communication that occurs in talking person-to-person. The digital age has assigned even more meaning to those brief periods when we actually talk to each other.

Is it disrespectful for a huge company's CEO who makes nine million dollars a year, or fifty-nine dollars a minute, to rush right past employees without saying, "Good morning?" That's about a three-dollar investment of the company money for him/her to say "hello." Is it worth it? If that CEO stands and talks for five minutes (or about three hundred dollars' worth of time), is it worth it? Respect is hard to define and just as difficult to measure. It can, however, result in impressive outcomes.

Powerful leaders must have a special measure of self-confidence and even a sense of entitlement to take on the enormous challenges of succeeding in the highly competitive business world. It takes a special audacity and over-the-top self-image to run a billion-dollar company. It also takes being able to spot the need for respect and dignity and the ability to act on that when necessary.

Any level of arrogance expressed by the big company CEO is not very becoming for a mid-level supervisor who thinks he/she will impress colleagues by being rude to a restaurant server while they're having lunch. There is a line between appropriate assertiveness and self-confidence to the point of unbearable arrogance.

A Look at Napoleon (of All People)

Consider the case of Napoleon Bonaparte. He is remembered as being one of the more arrogant leaders in history. Even as a youth, he had a disdain for weakness, writing in an essay at the age of seventeen, "Only the strong man is good; the weakling is evil."[1] Numerous historical sources say it was this arrogance and self-confidence that allowed him to lead 50 terribly violent and challenging battles within some twenty years.

Could one with any less confidence and even arrogance have personally led so many bloody battles in those tumultuous times? It was the arrogance that allowed him, with a force greatly outnumbered and facing a fortress town, to take Grenoble marching in with a song, rather than with swords drawn. It's the same arrogance that caused him, against huge odds, to abandon his exile at Elba.

One of the reasons he could lead fifty battles in twenty years, march into a heavily defended city singing, and have such a loyal following among so many troops and civilians was that Napoleon is said by many historians to have been very personable, respectful, considerate and even affectionate with those around him.

It was this showing of respect that caused him to be so loved that, when he was marching into Paris after abandoning his exile, he was taken up on the shoulders of a thousand people and escorted into the city with cheering crowds. It also meant that in his ultimate defeat, those officers around him offered their lives at close quarters to defend and extricate him from danger.

At the first of this chapter was the question: "Who do you think you are?" Are you someone whose colleagues would stand for your defense even in defeat? If the answer is "Yes," it's because you have chosen to communicate with your words, your body language and your actions in a way that has provided and earned respect.

It's difficult to define the strange balance between narcissism and humility that allows one to achieve what some may think impossible in leadership and have the graces to recognize the dignity of those in their company. This is a special quality in a leader that may not be recognized by superiors who are looking for short-term, careless and self-serving gains that only one with fully engaged narcissism might achieve.

In his extraordinary book *Getting Naked: A Business Fable About Shedding The Three Fears That Sabotage Client Loyalty*, Patrick Lencioni says long-lasting relationships are built on a willingness to be vulnerable and addresses the importance of revealing oneself.

> ...there is no better way to earn a person's trust than by

> putting ourselves in a position of unprotected weakness and demonstrating that we believe they will protect us.[2]

Graciousness with those around one in no way weakens, compromises, or challenges one's authority or opportunities for success. In fact, the impact is quite the opposite.

Leadership is not possible without trust. Management can be accomplished for a time through fear, but leadership demands trust. That quality only comes through mutual respect that is expressed in one's behavior, as well as one's language.

There is a marked trend running through corporations and business publications now focused on creating a kinder, gentler workplace. Business cultures are undergoing a shift away from the strictly short-term gain paradigm and are embracing a belief that long-term, stakeholder-focused gains with motivated, innovative employees can actually bring better shareholder value and more profitability.

There has been a recent flow of business articles and presentations underscoring this approach. Here are just few examples:

- Seven Ways to End Every Meeting On a Positive Note[3]
- Happy Workers, Richer Companies?[4]
- New Business Strategy: Treating Employees Well[5]
- Should Office Culture Change to Accommodate Introverts?[6]
- How GE Gives Leaders Time to Mentor and Reflect[7]
- Power Struggle? Why Your Top Performers Fight and What to Do About it[8]
- The CIA Has Suspended Its Iran Operations Chief Over his "Abusive" Management Style[9]

Ten years ago when this book was first written, it appeared company teams were trending toward more respectful, transparent, thoughtful and dignified interactions. Since then, a lot has happened, including the COVID isolation and a new political era of open hostility. Many just recently returned from home to live office working.

Bring to this the deep divisions developing among peoples and the advent of the influence and impersonal impact of AI, and it is difficult to say what corporate culture will become in the next five years.

Responsiveness

Coverage of business communication certainly would not be complete without a discussion of what is signaled by an individual's level of timely responsiveness to others. Time is a commodity. One can sell time to a company, but an individual only has so much of it. Everyone's time is in demand by something or someone, and for most people in the business world, it is stretched to a point of frustration and fatigue. Now that all of us as business people can move around great volumes of information and inquiries, the question of how we all use our time is confounding our interactions.

The value of time is reflected in our language. A person can spend time, save time, give up time, serve time, do time, take time and run out of time. It is a thing of value that everyone owns. It's also true that each person only owns a specific amount of time. That is true in a lifetime, in a day, in a week and in a moment. The working world, with all of the changes and demands described in this book, has compressed time into a maddening arena that rivals Wall Street for the frenzy with which we all set the prices in the market for the commodity of time.

Media outlets compete for it, employers demand it, families

long for it, and it frequently seems that no one's time is their own. In the midst of hundreds of emails, scores of text messages and a myriad of calls each day, most business people still operate with a fundamental belief that not being immediately responsive to someone's correspondence is a sign of disrespect. *The net result is that one is either forced to spend time because someone else has demanded it, or feel inadequate or guilty because he/she has not been responsive.*

Of course, the easy path for a communication book approaching the subject of responsiveness is to declare that not being responsive is a sign of disrespect. Unfortunately, it is no longer that simple. In some instances, sending communication that sets a recipient up to feel disrespectful if they don't spend *lots of time* answering is a show of disrespect in itself.

Earlier in this book, we talked about on-the-job bullying. In this era when people's work lives are frequently so harried and driven, *there is such a thing as time bullying*. That is disrespectfully, thoughtlessly and even cruelly forcing people to spend a valuable commodity of time in a way that is of little value. Success requires a deliberate and smart investment of time. *Time bullies can sidetrack the potential for success*. There is a need for respect in protecting someone's time in business, and a need to respectfully and appropriately offer one's valuable time to another.

Given the very complicated nature of the act of demanding time in the twenty-first-century business, it is an oversimplification to just say that anything other than an immediate response is disrespectful. One can say that responsiveness can sometimes buy responsiveness. Being responsive is a way of sending some very clear signals of respect. Here are some questions to ask when deciding how quickly and completely responsive one should be when receiving a communication:

- What is at stake here?
- How important is immediacy to the outcome?
- How important is my relationship with the person?
- How does this fit in my prioritization of time today?
- Does the timing of my response send some kind of signal to the initiator?
- Is there a specific signal I want to send with the timing of my response?
- Does it matter that I set a precedent for the level of responsiveness in the relationship?
- Is the time requirement for response reasonable?
- Is there a good way to shift the response to a better time?
- In what time frame does the person expect a response?
- Is it appropriate that the person expect a response?
- If this is time bullying, how do I appropriately push back?
- Do I want to contribute time to help this person in some way?

Overall one should err on the side of being helpful, compassionate and respectful in deciding on a level of responsiveness in any given situation. At the same time, there is just as much a need for respect in protecting someone's time in business as there is in appropriately offering time to another.

Just as a person doesn't just give their money away to anyone who asks for it, or even insist on having it, time is a valuable asset one should respectfully protect. In protecting every other valuable commodity in society, people expect to see boundaries, security and respect for possession and ownership.

One of the shortcomings of modern business is that most people have not learned to appropriately expect and give responsiveness in ways that respect the boundaries and finite nature of an individual's time. Despite the great value and limited quantity of our time as modern humans, it is one of the treasures most frequently and disrespectfully stolen away.

NINE

Filters, Scaffolds, Frames, and Uptalk

> If, as one people speaking the same language, they have begun to do this, then nothing they plan to do will be impossible for them. –,Genesis 11:6 NIV (Story of the Tower of Babel)

One might imagine making an impassioned presentation to people who are empathy-challenged, as described in the previous chapter, and not getting the expected empathetic response. There are so many variations to how speaking is understood and the response it may prompt that it sometimes seems rather miraculous that any dialogue takes place at all. How powerful would humankind become if we all had the same understanding of words, symbols and context?

Recently, I was helping an executive in his thirties prepare for a hearing in which billions of dollars were at stake. As he started his first practice attempt at the presentation, I was stunned to hear him lapse into what I refer to as "Uptalk."

"Oh my God," I said to my much younger colleague, "we have got to fix this guy's Uptalk, he sounds like a shallow novice. How did he allow himself to get to a place where he is talking like that?"

My colleague was silent. I had no way of knowing that she had no idea what I meant.

"I went home and looked it up," she told me weeks later. "I think you need to know there is a difference in generational understanding of what it signals when someone uses what you are calling 'Uptalk.'

This came as quite a surprise for someone who had been counseling for a number of years that speakers should get rid of this pattern in intonation. I had always known that it signaled inexperience, immaturity and lack of professionalism.

Politely, she informed me that my opinion may be skewed by a generational bias. Do you hate Uptalk? What characteristics about the speaker might it be signaling to you? Be careful, you may be saying something about the bias of your generation.

Uptalk, also known as "Upspeak," or, "High Rising Terminal" (HRT) that is a growing phenomenon that has worked its way around the English-speaking world.

It is characterized by an upswing in intonation at the end of a declarative sentence or a phrase, sounding almost like the ending of a question.

Early on in the United States, it was popularized in the media as being "Valley Girl Talk," referring to the dialect among teenage girls in the San Fernando Valley in California. Quickly, it spread to boys. Now I find women and men as old as their late thirties or early forties using it, even in quite formal professional settings.

In recent years, it has spread widely. Increasingly, I have encountered it coast to coast in the US and internationally among successful, influential, young business executives, some of them quite wealthy and successful. There is disagreement on Uptalk's origins, but it has apparently been around for a long time.

I realized I had found myself in a generational group that

despises the fact that a professional would use Uptalk. Not so apparent is that this generational difference is quite dramatic. Many professionals over forty or fifty years old have little appreciation for the important differences that can be found in an individual's interpretation of the symbolism or meaning of Uptalk. Surprisingly, both the groups that embrace the speech pattern and those who reject it are seldom aware that this difference exists.

What is known is quite varied. The speech pattern may have come to be viewed by the young as a sign of confidence and paternalism. Some researchers suggest Uptalk can occur in settings in which there may be a competition to hold the floor. "Floor holding" can play out in the sustained phrasing of the Uptalk cadence. The data are inconclusive, but it may signify to some audiences that the speaker is in control, is not finished and may preclude interruption.[1]

It would not be surprising that women, who have spent their lives being interrupted by men, would prefer a style that says, "don't interrupt me, I'm still talking." It is, then, understandable that executives of whatever gender would prefer what they might see as this more energetic, assertive approach, especially in dealing with other competitive young colleagues who know what the signaling of the intonation means.

As a communication consultant for some years, it has surprised me how many business people under forty I run into who have a hard time even recognizing the phenomenon of Uptalk. They also are quite surprised to be told that older persons may regard the dialect as signifying that the speaker is immature, undeveloped and shallow. Indeed, some older executives may make judgments of the speaker without ever realizing the meaning of the dialect to younger audiences.

The Uptalk reality is shifting rapidly. There is currently an awkward period when a thirty-something executive who is going to talk to a Board or regulatory body in which a large majority of the members are over fifty might want to give some thought to how their Uptalk is interpreted. This is especially true when it may be heard by those who are casting decisive votes on an important issue.

At the same time, an executive in a generational category that considers Uptalk a bad trait could miss out on the work, or advice, or brilliant contribution of a younger person whose dialect, when heard among their peers, is a mark of assertiveness, confidence and understanding.

What happens, then, if one is talking to a mixed-age or mixed-appreciation audience? Does one use Uptalk half the time? It's an interesting complication, but it gets more intricate. If younger people view Uptalk as denoting a vibrant, assertive, creative, intelligent person, what is the older, more traditional speaker actually conveying to those same young professionals while using a style the older speaker might think is a professional, authoritative, inspiring tone? As the population rapidly is skewing younger, we are beginning to have to cross this bridge.

It may very well be that as the Uptalk phenomenon becomes the norm (and surely it will), one can simply view the differences just like other dialect differences. Some small-minded persons will read stereotypical attributes into the dialect, but for most, the character, authenticity, intellect and content in the delivery will form the basis for identifying with the speaker.

The key here is that people hear with various filters, and we can't always trust them. Even a communication expert can be shocked to find that the ground has shifted and the meaning of sounds has changed.

The reference to Uptalk demonstrates again an important concept that listening takes place on several levels, and hearing is greatly influenced by what we are conditioned to hear. The closed mind may be a highly insulated mind that intakes quite a distorted version of reality.

We could cite a multitude of examples of generational/situational filtering in hearing. A dramatic one is the emergence of Rap music. To some Rap is simply a base line beat with someone talking over it. The differently-tuned ear hears only rhythm. The words are just part of the beat. Members of the Hip Hop culture who are followers of Rap hear something entirely different.

To say that Rap music, for example, could be moving, motivating, or inspirational may be quite surprising to some who hear it. Whether it divides along generational or societal lines, there is a hearing filter that sends a different signal to the brain for various listeners of Rap music.

Consider Examples from Rap

In their song *To Young Leaders,* Guante and Big Cats extol the virtues of doing over talking and building over just saying. It can be said that the works of artists like Guante and Big Cats, and Macklemore have sold millions of copies to fans who understand the lyrics. They convey pretty profound messages in a way that can be seen as generationally and attitudinally targeted to a specific type of audience.

While the beat might signal to a differently-tuned ear a feeling of anger, or angst, or disturbance, the presentations contain many important, even profound messages in the context in which they are being offered. Guante's idea, expressed in his music that "What you say is more important than how you say it," is offered with some very real context for the Rap enthusiasts.

Something to Hang It On

No good treatise about interaction would be complete without a discussion of the mental structure by which we understand our world.

The concept of "scaffolding" is generally used more in discussions about education than it is in business communication writings. That's because education is more generally understood as a construction process. It builds on layers of previously assimilated information and ideally would very deliberately put down new, additional levels of learning in a rather organized form.

At any moment, our reality is a product of layers of knowledge and experience that combine to create an understanding of our circumstances and input of information.

We consider this process of information access here in a business communication book because the concept provides a very good basis for understanding what takes place with scaffolding and communication in a business setting. By accessing the layers of reality that human beings' educational/experiential process has put in place new understandings are built on existing data.

One can compare the brain to a computer. Most computers have a certain amount of memory that's in place when they are turned on. The built-in resident memory tells the computer where to look for the hard drive and other parts necessary to access the higher-functioning memory storage. In much the same way, we are born with certain instincts that allow us to function at a fundamental level. These inherited instincts form the initial foundation for populating the more sophisticated memory built into our brains.

On this foundation, then, we build certain associations. For example, we as humans have associations related to touch, temperature, space and time. We learn that certain sounds lead to certain experiences, and that certain smells are associated with specific tastes. This is the foundation on which educational scaffolding builds our understanding of the world. It's also true that these sensory fundamentals serve as the reference point of all of the associations we make in the incredibly intricate layers of experience that constitute consciousness.

Building on the educated reference points we as humans assemble, we can take in billions of pieces of information in moments. Our thoughts have to sort through all of this to find meaning for our brains, with lightning speed, to decide what to do with that data. Some of this data may be categorized such that it's held briefly in short-term memory, some filed in long-term memory, and some simply discarded.

An example of this process would be if you were to feel some furry object rubbing against your leg. You begin to hang this on experiential data that's in place and associate the incoming data with some kind of animal. The touch helps you know it's friendly, that it is behaving in a certain way. The sight takes in the form of ears and tail, and you very quickly believe, based on your previous bank of experience and knowledge, that you have encountered a cat.

On the other hand, a little white stripe and a certain smell could change everything and signal that you have encountered a very friendly skunk. Seeing and smelling the skunk would access a different set of experiential memory and could create a very different response. One quick glimpse of a little white stripe would have dictated a different course of action for a response to the friendly creature.

Using the computer example, input has been received, memory has been accessed, data has been analyzed and output has been achieved. Like the computer comparison, information must be labeled and filed appropriately for this mental computation to function properly.

Suppose you are working in a word processing program

and want to save a file. There is a very specific procedure for this. You must have created a file folder with a label and a name for your file. There can, in fact, be quite an array of folders and subfolders, but each one must be specifically labeled and accessed according to the right procedure.

If this is not done, your file will be rejected or end up in the wrong place. The hierarchical file structure in the computer is the scaffold containing data that has been sorted, labeled and indexed, layer on layer, as memory is acquired and ultimately made accessible to the end user.

The theories of scaffolding suggest that the brain works in much the same way as a computer. So, having the appropriate label on data has an impact on the efficiency, accuracy and specificity with which information is received (or whether it is received at all). This suggests that putting information in context as one dispenses it dramatically improves the potential for appropriate processing of that data.

It's All About Context, but Whose?

Think of the intricate context and layers of understanding that might need to be in place if one were to start describing their contact lenses to someone at a party. They might give the prescription strength in detail, the brand, the type, the tint. They could tell when they got the contacts and what type they might be. Suppose also that the real goal is to find a lost contact.

One would want to, instead, initially give the context that, "I have dropped a contact lens, would you just stand still a moment and glance around for it?" Now the prescription strength is of little interest. If they were with people who understand what contact lenses are, they simply might want to say where it may have fallen. (If with a rare group of aboriginal Amazonian tribal people who have never heard of contact lenses, one might have another kind of communication challenge on their hands entirely.)

Suppose, on the other hand, one were to say, "I just knocked out my contact lens trying to get away from a rattlesnake loose in this room. Can you help me find it?" Now some very powerful, core instincts would be invoked and prompt a pretty dramatic and different response.

Good dialogue may, then, be characterized by how well we can access the existing mental scaffolding to convey data in a way that is best understood and even embraced by the recipient. We would want to make sure that the information is framed in such a way that it's filed by the recipient with labels that appropriately represent the mutual context both, the originator and the recipient, have agreed should be assigned to the data.

In order to facilitate a better interaction, a new "file folder" and a new "label" often must be generated when conveying additional layers of information. Examining our dialogue in consideration of this reality, we would suggest that one must clearly label information in a mutually understood context.

The various branches of the United States Military promote a communication style referred to as *"BLUF" (Bottom Line Up Front)*. The approach emphasizes getting the important context in place before the details of a communication are added. The US Navy even has a blog publication titled *Bottom Line Up Front*. The concept is an integral part of assuring that there is a crisp, understandable relay of information in all the various forms of communication and that a label is in place before additional data are distributed.

All of human consciousness has core reference points in our sensory experience. Sensory associations influence in very powerful ways the processing of information. This is so apparent it can be measured.

A 2008 study by Williams and Bargh demonstrated that

brief exposure to physical warmth or coldness alters people's social perceptions and behaviors as well. Study subjects who briefly held a cup of hot coffee judged an ambiguous person to whom they were exposed as having a "warmer" personality (e.g., more generous, sociable and friendly). Participants who held a cup of iced coffee judged the ambiguous person to be more "cool" (less generous and more antisocial).[2]

Any good, experienced educator knows that a cluttered room, an uncomfortable temperature, or an empty stomach can interfere with learning much like static can garble a radio signal. It's also true that drawing on the instinctive operational functions of our mental computer, actual time and space sensory anchoring can impact how we assess a concept.

Meier and Robinson found evidence in a study that the determination of the positive or negative implication of words is impacted by where the words are displayed on a computer screen. When study subjects saw a positive word in the upper half of the screen, they processed it more quickly than they did the same positive word presented in the lower half of the screen.[3]

Clearly, when we establish dialogue, we are working through layer after layer of this mental context established over years of collecting data by both persons involved in a conversation. These layers of information are comprised of sensory, as well as other experiential and linguistic data.

Even as a seasoned communication professional, I had gone through years of being absolutely convinced that I knew exactly what Uptalk was and how it impacted one's communicating in all audiences. It took a re-labeling with new context and new convincing data for me to change this frame by which I had understood Uptalk.

In a very real way, *our* world can only be *my* world because it is only in the context of the world that has been structured in my brain that I can understand anything.

Whether one calls it *"Framing," "Key Messaging," "Context," "Thesis Sentence,"* or *"Bottom Line Up Front,"* we must acknowledge a necessity to find a clear mutual basis on which we can structure the connotation of any further communication. We must make the appropriate connections with what we already know and accommodate each participant's scaffolding of previous learning as we enter into a specific dialogue.

In this context, it could be argued that almost anyone could learn almost anything if it's given in small enough pieces and ties appropriately to what they already know.

Analogies work well to convey complicated concepts because they anchor to knowledge and context that already exists to explain something new. For example, I just used the analogy of a computer to discuss brain function. The comparison, building and reinforcement aspects of scaffolding in learning is one of the reasons kids can watch a movie six times and learn something new every time.

In Search of a Frame

> To be accepted, the truth must fit people's frames. If the facts do not fit a frame, the frame stays and the facts bounce off. – George Lakoff[4]

For there to be meaningful dialogue, there must be a mutual reference point for that dialogue. We as humans see things in the context of frames. Framing is the mental packaging, or file folder labeling, that human brains undertake to chunk information into various categories.

If, for example, one were to mention the word "violin," it would trigger a violin frame in thinking that could then influence all else that is said about a violin. The word "fiddle" would probably trigger an entirely different frame, even though they may refer to the same instrument. The idea of saying someone played a violin in a bluegrass music band might trigger conflicting frames.

Another example of a frame is the word "hula." Consider the frame context that comes into play when that word is mentioned, and a grass skirt comes to mind. When I hear "hula hoop," however, I have thoughts of childhood.

If one has a frame that clowns are frightening (perhaps based on some movie or childhood experience), any effort to provide that person with a happy, lighthearted experience of clowns is going to somehow require some new framing. In fact, the thought of clowns as scary is a relatively new meme, promoted primarily by Hollywood.

For many years, the concept of framing was associated with a negative connotation of manipulative media influence in directing the categorization of our thoughts. People are so saturated with media in this century and have so many frames in our minds as a result of years of media exposure, we have come to a point of docile acceptance that frames are formed in a multitude of ways and probably (in our time) mostly involving the electronic media.

We Name Our World to Own and Control It

Humankind has undertaken the great task of placing a name on everything in the known universe, down to its tiniest particles. In fact, it could be said that the known universe is only the named universe. It's through this naming that we possess, control, experience and assign a reality to our surroundings.

Through this naming, humans presume to claim a kind of ownership of all named things. It's through this naming that we share the experience of the owned world with our peers. Many of the names become associated with frames that organize our consciousness and make information retrievable in our brains. The naming and ownership through naming also serve to reinforce feelings of security. We feel safer when we believe we name, understand and claim the universe around us.

Not only do we name everything, we also come up with acronyms. Segments of the business world are full of acronyms by which we sift out unknowing persons and create the elite and clandestine ownership of data. Medical researchers, for example, must know LOCF (Last Observation Carried Forward) or ITT (Intent to Treat Population). If one is engaged in reviewing pharmaceutical documents and doesn't know that OTC stands for "Over the Counter," they can immediately be labeled a novice.

It gets even more challenging because every field in medical research has its own additional set of acronyms. Oncologists, cardiologists, cardioelectrophysiologists, etc. all speak their own acronym language. One can add to that the flurry of acronyms accompanying related pharmacodynamic and other scientific input into drug development, and the language becomes very challenging.

Then, to submit a drug for approval by the government requires an entirely different set of regulatory language. Now there is layer after layer of difficult terms that must be known as acronyms and as their full names in order to participate in the dialogue that would ultimately get a drug approved for use. This pattern is repeated in thousands of areas of expertise in people's business lives.

The naming, owning through naming and obscuration provided by acronyms is a great differentiator that elevates status and forms the perception of knowledge and authority in thousands of professions.

Mislabeling in a complicated world can lead to disastrous results. One can look at a simple example that has been popularized as an urban legend in social media. The story tells of an unfortunate parent who is struggling to try to keep up on social media with his daughter, who is away for her first year at college. This person somehow gets the idea that "LOL" stands for "Lots of Love." The daughter, on the other hand, knows that, in social media language, "LOL" means "Laughing Out Loud." Being a loving parent the Dad distributes "LOL" generously in his tweets. Here is an exchange:

> Hey Dad, I'm really homesick and miss you guys terribly

> We both say LOL! Hope that will help a little with getting through it. What else can we do?

> Seriously Dad, I am all alone cause my roommate is gone to her grandmother's funeral

> Oh, tell her LOL from your mother and me! Also, we just can't quit thinking about your situation. Let me say again, LOL !

One fundamental difference in the understanding of a strategic symbol here causes some big problems in this exchange.

The Astounding Process of Human Understanding

It's hard to imagine the magnitude of brain processing into which one interjects the complicated and multifaceted messages that one would expect people to receive, process and understand in context. New scientific examination is shedding more light on just how incredible is this process of the human mind.

In 2013, researchers from the Riken HPCI Program for

Computational Life Sciences, the Okinawa Institute of Technology Graduate University (OIST) in Japan, and Forschungszentrum Jülich in Germany carried out a huge neuronal network simulation.

In a process that took forty minutes to complete, they were able to achieve the simulation of one second of neuronal network activity in real, biological time.

This team succeeded in simulating a network consisting of 1.73 billion nerve cells connected by 10.4 trillion synapses. To realize this feat, the program recruited 82,944 processors of a system (K) that is at the RIKEN Kobe campus. In a news release, the team revealed:

> Although the simulated network is huge, it only represents 1% of the neuronal network in the brain. The nerve cells were randomly connected, and the simulation itself was not supposed to provide new insight into the brain - the purpose of the endeavor was to test the limits of the simulation technology developed in the project and the capabilities of K. In the process, the researchers gathered invaluable experience that will guide them in the construction of novel simulation software.
>
> ...simulating a large neuronal network and a process like learning requires large amounts of computing memory. Synapses, the structures at the interface between two neurons, are constantly modified by neuronal interaction, and simulators need to allow for these modifications.
>
> More important than the number of neurons in the simulated network is the fact that during the simulation, each synapse between excitatory neurons was supplied with 24 bytes of memory. This enabled an accurate mathematical description of the network. In total, the simulator coordinated the use of about 1 petabyte of main memory, which corresponds to the aggregated memory of 250,000 PCs.[5]

Remember all of that undertaking is involved to run the equivalent of one second of human thought. Imagine the processing that has to go on when we give a three-minute answer to someone's simple question. The chances for misperception or misconnection of ideas are enormous.

Despite complicated mental processing, humans believe we are able to conduct successful activities of interaction and communication much of the time. The haunting truth is that this isn't as accurate and successful as we sometimes think, and that context, framing and specificity become quite important if we want to be clearly understood

The result of the labeling, naming and claiming we humans do is that we create increasingly complicated bases for establishing context for our interactions. It's also true, however, that to have meaningful interactions, accessing this context is vital. In other words, we must use terms that are understood in the same way by all parties of the dialogue.

Tips for Meaningful Dialogue - Creating Clarity

All these findings of how people come to understand information imply there are several necessities for establishing a meaningful dialogue. They include:

- Determine the mutual reference data and frames upon which the communication will be established.
- Spell out in a clear and concise way the basis/premise for the communication, clearly labeling the mental "folders/subfolders" in which

the information will be placed before streaming data.

- Convey the data of the communication in a way that includes mutually established/understood terms, symbols, language and communication form and style.
- Provide data in a way that is crisp, focused and is the essence of the message.
- Confirm the clarity of the exchange and its meaning and interact to make sure the proper frames have been applied.

Not so easy? The complicated arena we maneuver for meaningfully communicating is also not a friendly territory for presumption. It should be quite obvious at this point that effective dialogue means caring enough to tune in, to listen, to explore, ask questions and understand the common basis for communication.

That kind of understanding doesn't happen much in this busy, heavily digital world. Little wonder there is so much generalization, division, misunderstanding and missed opportunities for meaningful dialogue

TEN

The Integrity of Proof

> "If it doesn't fit, you must acquit." – Johnnie Cochran, attorney in the OJ Simpson trial

There is an enormous amount of human communication that is dependent upon a presumption of trust. Can what a speaker is saying be trusted as true? The matter of what constitutes proof is a source of a good deal of misunderstanding in business. The ability to apply the concept properly can enhance interpersonal relations, internal and external business interactions, credibility and even sales. Unfortunately, too many people get it wrong because they are too naïve or biased in their pronouncements of what they believe to be proof.

There are some fundamental perceptions of reality that most business people are pretty sure they understand quite well. They believe, for example, that they know what "truth" is. There is, however, irony in the fact that the concept of "truth" as most people use the word in everyday language has to depend on some confusing circular thinking.

- We all generally understand truth to be that which is true. It's supported by accepted facts.
- At the same time, facts are those things that are accepted as actual, real and true.
- Facts, being accepted as what is real and true, then become proof.
- Proof helps us accept what is truth.

On the other hand, proof is only evidence of truth if it is accepted as true.

If you caught a lot of "accepted" and "accept" in the previous sentences, you're catching on. The bottom line is that truth is what we understand to be true, based on facts that we believe to be true, such that it becomes proof that is accepted as true. In fact, mathematicians could work this out in rooms full of blackboards and still have lots of calculating to do to prove truth.

Truth could be a concept quite different for an attorney than it might be for a statistician. Statistical proof might go a long way in a pharmaceutical hearing, but it would seldom be applied in a criminal courtroom.

Absolute Truth?

One might protest that there are absolute truths. Maybe we could point to scripture or math. The question becomes "Whose scripture, whose math and whose measure of belief serves as the basis for the 'absolutes'." (Oh and a statistician would ask, "Have the results been tested for multiplicity?") Even statisticians are disturbed by a popularly held misperception that reaching a traditionally convincing statistical p-value of .05 constitutes statistical "proof." In this case, even math and statistics can be challenged.

One can even reference color to claim truth. "It's as clear as black and white," we might say, but a black-and-white-striped wheel (called a Benham Wheel) turning at certain speeds can yield a rainbow of color. Or one might say, "It's true blue," but blue may appear, relative to the depth of clear water, or the distance one is from green grass.

Of course, this can get quite complicated. We could become embroiled in examining a philosophical approach, a mathematical approach, or even a metaphysical approach to addressing what constitutes proof.

We will stick with a communication approach that simply says:

> Proof is that which verifies a matter as true in the minds of the receivers of a communication. This is not to say that proof isn't achievable in all of the aforementioned arenas. In our usual communication, we simply must make sure that the truth being proven is considered in light of several questions:

- Truth to whom?
- From what source?
- How much evidence is there?
- In what context is the evidence provided?
- To what level of specificity?
- What kind of reliable verification is there?
- What are the filters for understanding the facts?
- How much is at stake in consideration of the proof?
- What is the trust level and acceptance?

We should keep in mind that trust and risk are important factors in determining how specific a proof must be to sufficiently convince a recipient.

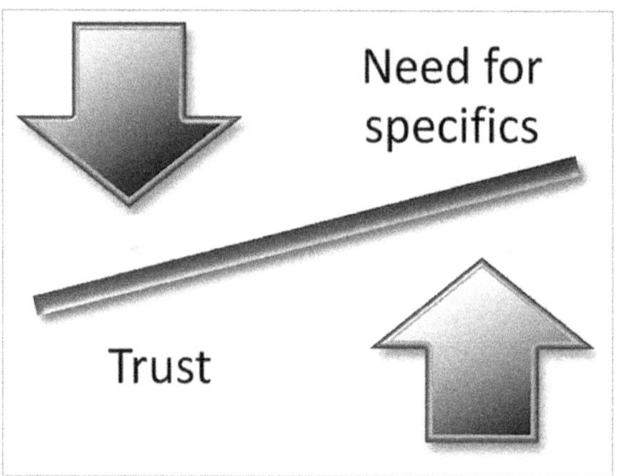

As the trust level goes down, the need for specificity in the proof will go up. Also, when the perception of what's at stake (risk) goes up, the need for specificity will go up.

In other words, when the trust is low and the stakes/risks run high, one had better be able to offer some specific, clearly stated, validated proof.

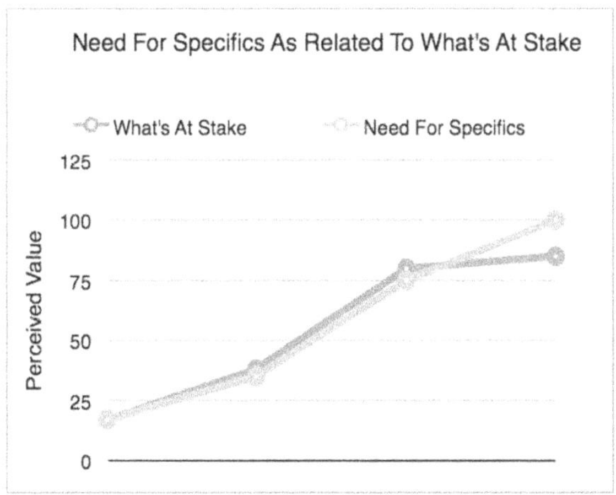

As an example, consider the teenager who is supposed to be home at 10:00 PM. If a reliable teen calls a parent to say he/she is with their grandparents and will be "home in a little while," the risk may be perceived to be low and the trust level high. In that case some generalized explanation might suffice for parental acceptance of a later arrival at home.

If, however, a teen calls to say he/she is at a party with a group of newly-met twenty-somethings, but "I'm not drinking and will be home in a while," the risk could be considered to be higher, and the trust level for all concerned could go down. The need for specificity would be rather heavily increased.

Let's add another layer and say there is a tornado warning in the area at the time of the call, and location services on the phone says this teen is not where she/he says they are. Now, risk level has surged enormously, trust level has dropped precipitously and the demand for specifics has probably just taken a dramatic turn.

Now the parent is probably not only searching for specificity and car keys, but for verification. When the trust level takes a big drop, even the specificity can come under scrutiny. It then takes an even stronger and more independent verification to recover credibility.

Verification takes on an entirely new meaning when trust is down and the stakes are high. A common mistake in attempting to communicate ideas is to misunderstand the recipient's perception of the level of trust and what is at stake. Another common mistake is to assume that very specific public or private anxiety can be soothed with broad and philosophical generalities.

Anyone seeking to examine the delicate thread on which truth hangs need only go through the transcripts of thousands of hours of United States Food and Drug Administration Advisory Committee hearings in which drugs and devices, fully scientifically tested in controlled clinical trials, are further questioned for the presence of proof of safety and efficacy of a product. In these hearings life or serious adverse events may loom as risks.

It may come as a surprise to some that there is very rarely a decision made in such a setting without some outstanding challenges having to do with statistics, application of the sciences, or computational assumptions remaining unresolved.

Here one learns that proof, chance and presumption exist in a strange, interactive cloud of acceptance of the methods and levels of verification judged as acceptable in relationship to the risks involved.

Can I Get a Witness?

Nowhere is truth on trial more than in a criminal or civil court case. Jurors actually discuss the same evidence, then take a vote. There is little question that the experience of the jurors weighs heavily on their interpretation of the evidence that has been presented to them. Attorneys can spend hours qualifying witnesses to try to discover what in their background or experience could have influenced their interpretation of the evidence presented in a case.

Judges will instruct jurors to remain impartial and not let personal experiences weigh into their decision-making of a case. While the vast majority of people ready to serve on the jury will agree to and believe they are following the judge's instructions, it is virtually impossible for one to disassociate themselves from their experiences.[1]

The closer a potential juror's experiences are to facts surrounding the case the more likely one side or the other (or both sides) would not want that person to serve on the jury in an attempt to maintain a more "neutral" interpretation of the facts. Liz Thompson, a litigation consultant for over eighteen years and President of TL Consulting, a company of experts on jury selection, puts it this way:

> How then can one say that the truth was reached when two sides are arguing different interpretations of some of the same facts? The hope is that the six-to-twelve jurors selected are as neutral as possible, that the credibility of the witnesses are examined along with the information provided by those witnesses and that the sum of all the facts provided by either side lend to the jury finding one side has the greater weight of the evidence (for civil cases) or beyond the shadow of a doubt (for criminal) is "the truth."[2]

Interpretation of truth can have far-reaching consequences in business communication. From pharmaceuticals to nuclear operations, from water systems to telephone companies, it is common for corporate witnesses in those organizations to be frequently called before committees and commissions to defend company activities and ambitions and tell the truth.

Also common to all of those cases is that they file hundreds of thousands, if not millions, of pages of data, evidence and pre-filed testimony. Even with all of that data and scores of computer files full of evidence, people are called to be seated on a stand, sworn in and to give live testimony for their cause. Why? What is it that creates the situation in which mountains of data might be trumped by a few hours of in-person questioning of a company witness or outside expert? The live hearings are all simply a quest for meaning that adds context to all of the mountains of data.

Patient Outcomes

Looking, for example, at a US Food and Drug Administration Advisory Committee hearing, one can see this quest for meaning play out in case after case. There may be hours of debate and argument over statistical analysis and methods of data collection. The data are powerful and persuasive, but they can create confusion without someone to bring meaning to the argument. What is the clinical significance, the proper perspective on patient outcomes, the true meaning of improvement in the quality of life that results from the treatment? What is the clinician's experience in using the treatment? How does the doctor think it all fits in the armamentarium of medications or devices? In assessing the benefit/risk, how well can one define the benefit in the very challenging matter of hard-to-quantify patient responses? The sorting of truth and meaning becomes paramount.

Remember, truth is what people accept as true, based on proof that they accept as valid. This is colored by how much is perceived to be at stake and how much one trusts the presenter. This matter of trust is the vital piece of the equation. If company witnesses violate this bond of trust in such a hearing, convincing the governing body of proof takes on an entirely different level of challenge.

What Does It All Mean?

The next understanding to consider is the difference between truth and meaning. A truth, or collection of truths, or even a collection of impressions, can result in an ultimate perception of meaning. Sociology and Philosophy scholar Hannah Arendt says it clearly:

> ...and truth and meaning are not the same. The basic fallacy, taking precedence over all specific metaphysical fallacies, is to interpret meaning on the model of truth.[3]

This difference between truth and meaning is one of the primary reasons regulatory bodies have public hearings. After all the data are presented and issues discussed, a determination must be made as to what it all means in reference to some desired outcome. The presenter who can work through all of the data and ultimately provide meaning is frequently the one who carries the day.

Because truth and proof seem elusive and so reliant on context and meaning, the integrity of those with influence becomes an important factor. When such persons and organizations sway great numbers of the population and enormous spheres of activity and productivity, their integrity in recognizing or shaping truth and proof is critical. Intentionally undermining society for selfish purposes by manipulating meaning is one of the more sinister powers in the digital age.

This brings us to the matter of Artificial Intelligence and truth. We live in a time of "deep fake," where seeing is not necessarily believing. A chat prompt may not always be trusted to bring verifiable facts. The responsibility remains with you as an originator to provide as much verification as possible when you disseminate data. It is an increasingly challenging expectation.

INTEGRITY

The delicate thread on which one's understanding of truth and trust may hang is the best argument for the practice of personal integrity in business. It's not in the words that are spoken, but in the trustworthiness with which one carries out business commitments, the respect with which one treats others and the commitment to make sure communication is conducted in the context of what one believes to be true that trust is built for convincing interaction.

The bottom line for all of us as communicators is that my truth can only be your truth if we share the same confidence in the basis for trust and meaning. It is seldom in one's own speaking, but in periods of silence, hearing and discerning of context that one gets an understanding of how to provide convincing proof and meaning to a given audience.

> There are no facts, only interpretations. – Friedrich Nietzsche

> Everything we hear is an opinion, not a fact. Everything we see is a perspective, not the truth. – Marcus Aurelius

ELEVEN

Hear and Heal

> I heard no small voices and you didn't either," and the small kangaroo in her pouch said, 'me neither.' – Dr. Seuss, *Horton Hears A Who*[1]

Sometimes we, as modern humans, all suffer from attention deprivation. That is, no one gives us enough attention. In a world in which we have billions of pieces of data coming in and an enormous amount going out, it can frequently seem like we are not being heard at all. Too often, we're involved in conversations where no one is hearing because they are too busy thinking about what they're going to say. Successfully communicating in the twenty-first century will increasingly have to involve doing a lot of hearing.

It seems that in business writings, there is quite a lot of focus now on *listening*. While articles about listening dominate business literature, there isn't much written about *hearing*, and there is a difference.

A handful of leadership development writers promote a message that it's a great leadership attribute to be able to quietly listen to subordinates. Unfortunately, many of these articles place little emphasis on what one does with what one hears. Hearing with purpose and authentic investment in the heard is quite rare indeed. Turning the herd in business into the heard is a substantial undertaking.

With the enormous amount of attention given recently in the leadership development business to the matter of "listening," it's important to further draw the distinction that listening isn't hearing. Very early in my career, I earned some college tuition by working as a proud, young, ambitious radio announcer.

We at the station always waited anxiously to see the latest ratings to find out how many "listeners" we had. As the ratings increased, my perception of power and influence grew. I entertained myself with the thought that thousands of people were hanging onto my every word.

It wasn't until later in life, as a casual radio listener myself, that I discovered that listening to the radio isn't always hearing the radio. My assumption of being heard by all of the hundreds of thousands who were counted as listeners was grossly overblown.

Consider a comparison of listening and profound hearing. Listening generally involves one tuning into a speaker in the context of the listener's own frames (as discussed in the earlier chapter that covered framing). Profound hearing comes with a willingness to suspend the listener's own frames to search for and try to understand the frames of the speaker. The choice of the word "profound" is made to suggest the potential for profound understanding of context from which the speaker is expressing opinions.

Here, in *profound hearing,* emerges the potential for a listener to even form new frames. Here is a fertile ground for the sharing of innovative ideas, as well as a solid affirmation of mutual perceptions as the interaction progresses. One can listen for hours using only one's own set of frames and never hear the reality of the context in which the speaker is presenting information.

This is the risk in deciding that forcing oneself to listen is an admirable characteristic of leadership. A mark of an innovative leader is the ability to have enough fluidity in their own framing to tune into the frames of others. In many cases, such hearing can also give a greater understanding of the emotions of others.

Discussions about listening seldom touch on the power that resides in the act of having been heard. People are powerfully longing to be heard, and we all have something to say. Is anyone hearing?

In 2003, a group named Story Corps set up a recording booth in Grand Central Station in New York City. They invited anyone to walk in and conduct an extended recorded interview with a friend, relative, or even a stranger. Participants were promised a free CD of their interview and agreed to allow the interview to be archived.

The results were striking, with people willing and happy to take the process seriously and conduct revealing, even intimate and moving interviews. The project was so successful it has now resulted in setting up recording booths in cities across America and is spreading internationally. Story Corps suggested questions like:

- When in life have you felt most alone?
- If you could hold on to one memory from your life forever, what would that be?
- How has your life been different from what you'd imagined?
- How would you like to be remembered?
- Do you have any regrets?
- What does your future hold?
- Of what are you most proud

The project has recorded about a hundred thousand interviews. This oral record of hearing is being stored in the Library of Congress Archives.

In 2008, Story Corps started the National Day of Listening on the day after Thanksgiving in the US to encourage people to listen to each other and to participate in the Story Corps online program to conduct and listen to interviews with family and friends. The success of the program demonstrates that many people have something to say, that there is a great need to be heard, and an underlying hope that something an individual says will make a difference to someone somewhere.

The Power of Having Been Heard

Discussed here will be not just listening, but paying attention, actively hearing and the impact of the act of having been heard. In fact, what we call "paying" attention is actually that. It's an investment in another. It comes at a cost of our time and the valuable commodity of our concentration. It also has to come with the listener investing enough trust to be interested in the frames in which the speaker understands information.

The recipient of this experience of *having been heard* can actually be enriched by the exchange with immeasurable rewards. The concentration and effort toward understanding all of the elements of another's discourse is the great difference between listening and hearing.

The title of this book, *You Are What You Don't Say: Finding a New Paradigm in Business Communication,* makes reference to those defining moments people take to listen, observe, invest, understand context, enhance relationships and make certain that the words they then speak have meaning and value.

Having someone hear you, truly hear you, is one of the most rare, affirming, enhancing and healing experiences one can have. There is a specific human emotion in having been heard. Healing through hearing is a much researched, powerful elixir, yet this is a fast-moving world where people too often deprive each other of the gift of that healing power of affirmation of humanity, importance and individuality. A consideration of the importance of affirmation of being heard also speaks of the growing dangers of the use of detached, digital texting that encourages more listening than hearing. Deprivation of this power of having been heard is a major contribution to illness and anxiety.

This subject of the act of being heard would seem to be an area for quite a lot of fruitful research and discussion. There are some studies being conducted that examine the impact that access to the internet has had on feelings of additional empowerment for groups of people who may have previously considered themselves deemed less powerful in society.

For example, research in 2009 found that women are more likely than men to create blogs. In fact, further research in 2012 seemed to substantiate that the act of being heard in the form of blogging brought an increased perception of having a competent, confident, assertive voice, or "Sense of Agency" to female bloggers. In addition, there was an increase in the area of "Sense of Community," the sense of empowerment in the ability to enter into dialogue with others. A study by Carmen Stavrositu and S. Shyam Sundar, suggests there is a potential for blogging to additionally empower women in many ways.[2]

The study also demonstrated that this additional empowerment from having been heard may well be experienced even when there is no instant feedback or accurate estimate of how large the audience or who the hearers are.

The internet has, in fact, provided a platform for enrichment and empowerment for any number of societal factions that otherwise would not have the opportunity to be heard on such a scale as the web provides. The web, of course, does not always provide the individual user with metrics on who is hearing. To some extent, the assumption that someone is out there paying attention may be all that is needed to trigger the enriching power of having been heard.

Increasingly, parents are being schooled on the character and social-enhancing empowerment that children experience through the act of having been heard.

In a 2002 press release entitled *Why Children Must Be Heard,* UNICEF announced results of a study it says confirms that being heard can be a powerful contributor to childhood development around the world. The report notes that:

> Listening to the opinions of children does not mean simply endorsing their views; rather, engaging them in dialogue and exchange allows them to learn constructive ways of influencing the world around them. The social give and take of participation encourages children to assume increasing responsibilities as active, tolerant and democratic citizens in formation.[3]

In 2012, researchers from the Massachusetts Institute of Technology published a study that looked at the result of a perception of having been heard on the part of groups considered less empowered. In the first study of its kind on what authors called "perspective giving" (the opportunity to share one's own story with someone else) the researchers sought to determine whether the less empowered group would benefit more from perspective giving than perspective taking. In other words, was there a restorative quality to the circumstance of one's story having been heard.

To test the hypothesis, Palestinians and Israelis and Mexican immigrants and white Arizonans, were recruited. The Arizona study was conducted six months after the passage of a controversial anti-immigration bill. The Middle East study was conducted six months after the 2009 Israeli military action in Gaza.

The study found evidence that the experience of writing one's own stories to be read by a dominant group improves attitudes toward the dominant group more than hearing comments from the dominant group.

In a questionnaire given before and after the interaction, attitudes toward the opposing group improved most among members of the disempowered group who told their own stories and among members of the dominant group who read others' stories. The research reinforces an idea of a unifying and restorative power that comes from the experience of having been heard.

Previous studies in similar exchanges have shown that the dominant group often ends up doing more of the talking. The argument could be made that it could be more powerful and more persuasive to hear people give their perspective, rather than to make statements to them.[57]

What has not been tested in these studies is what would be the outcomes if the perception of having been heard could be confirmed in feedback from the hearer that demonstrated they got the message.

> Listen to me, please just now, that's all I ask of you. – David E. Jones, *A Soldier's Story: The Power of Words*[4]

Are We Asking the Right Questions?

Powerful hearing is usually sustained by good questions. Statements can render sweeping declarations and quotable opinions, but it's questions that change the world. The right questions can ignite thoughts that may never have been found otherwise.

Some years ago, I had the experience of having one question change my life. I was considering going to graduate school quite a long time after getting my undergraduate degree. Traveling extensively and working full-time as a consultant, I knew that it would be a challenge. Wrestling with the thoughts of mixing with much younger students, contending with an education system I hadn't seen in years, and having to drive eighty miles round-trip to class and back, I was anxious and undecided.

Fortunately, I had a dear friend Jeannette (who is mentioned earlier in this book) who had taught college for years and knew education well. At eighty-eight years old, she had taught high school until retirement, then taught college for another thirty years, and was still teaching. If anyone could tell me whether going back to school was a good idea, it would be Jeannette.

I called with the thought that she could give me a long dissertation on the whys and why-nots of graduate school at my age. After a rather lengthy detailing of all my concerns, I finally asked what she thought of the idea.

She simply answered with a question: "Well, honey, what else are you going to do with the remaining fifty or sixty years of your life?" The question had a powerful impact. It changed the course of my life for all the years since, gave me an entirely different perspective on aging and created a rather tireless quest to live those "fifty or sixty years" with purpose.

At the original writing of this book in 2016, Jeannette was a hundred and one, and still brilliant, healthy, and going strong, providing a wonderful model for the answer she gave to my question.

~

People used to work in a marketplace where questioning wasn't necessary for most of the workforce. The die was cast, the blueprint was issued, or the edict was handed down, and a hierarchical system dictated a mundane course of productive labor for millions of workers. In a business world where trends change at lightning speed and there is a high premium on innovation, questions are imperative for business survival. With a growing number of businesses that practice distributed leadership, appropriate questioning is vital.

In recent years, a growing emphasis on asking what are called "Clean Questions" is finding a place in business. Originally a concept based in psychotherapy, Clean Questioning is designed to get behind the usual expected exchanges and help people in conversation trigger new thinking and access to hidden, obscured, or suppressed thinking that wouldn't otherwise surface.

"Clean" questions would generally be open-ended, including how, what, where, when and/or who, would include words/language from the other person's previous comments, and be open-ended probes for exploration and learning.

A well-known neurolinguistic programming expert, Sue Knight, describes clean questions as being "naïve, present, open, not knowing, alert, aware, fascinated, eager to learn and selfless."[5] Whatever one may call them, we need more questions like that in our world right now.

Forgetting How to Ask

In his book *A More Beautiful Question*, journalist Warren Berger makes a strong case that the United States is producing a non-questioning generation because of an educational system where questioning by students is suppressed.

Berger quotes a number of research sources to demonstrate that as children rise higher in grade level, they become less and less questioning and are allowed to ask fewer and fewer questions.[6]

Thomas Dee and Hans Henrik Sieversten have conducted a definitive study among a large group of school children in which they produced convincing evidence that delaying the children's start in school for one year dramatically reduced inattention and hyperactivity at age seven and that the results persisted when measured again at age eleven.[7] Perhaps one more important hypothesis is that a little more time for inquiry and exploration before regimentation and suppression of curiosity could help solve what is an epidemic of attention deficit.

One great ray of hope in the matter of children being willing and able to question in education is an organization called the Right Question Institute (http://rightquestion.org) that has been put together by educators who have recognized this problem of suppression of curiosity. The group champions the cause of teaching questioning skills. It focuses on a technique called The Right Question (RQ) strategy that teaches two foundational skills:

- How to formulate questions (Taught through a "Question Formulation Technique" that they offer free)
- How to focus on decisions and use specific criteria for accountable decision-making (by using a "Framework for Accountable Decision-Making")

Members of the organization claim that, despite their significance, these skills are rarely explicitly taught. They have designed simple methods to help individuals learn them and then teach others. An institute publication lists some examples of what happens when the RQ Strategy is taught to people who have never had the opportunity to learn to ask their own questions and focus on key decisions that affect them:

• Women in an **adult literacy** program in New Hampshire learn to advocate for themselves and secure better job training opportunities through their local welfare office.

• Patients in **community health center**s in the Bronx and Brooklyn, NY learn to ask questions and participate in decisions made during their encounters with health care providers

• Immigrant **parents** in New Mexico begin to ask questions about how to help prevent violence in their children's schools and eventually organizing into a powerful local force to improve opportunities and outcomes for all children.

• **Sugar cane plantation workers** in Hawaii, about to lose the sole source of livelihood, learn to ask questions and participate in decisions about how to use the land for different purposes, supporting small businesses and begin to have a say in decisions about how company-owned housing will be allocated.

• Residents in a **homeless shelter** in Louisville, KY, discover the value of having a say in the school assignment process and become effective advocates for their children entering middle schools across the city.

• **Teachers** in England tweet about the changes they see in their students. The teachers read an article about the Question Formulation Technique and immediately implemented it in their classrooms and found their students more engaged and stimulated to think in new ways than they had ever before."[8]

Business could do well to embrace some of the fundamentals of the organization's approach. The institute has offered the Question Formulation Technique for public distribution, and we reproduce it here with encouragement that readers contribute to and support the organization. We also bring it to the attention of the business community that, just like much of education, it requires a renewed understanding of the power of questioning.

This has been driven home in recent years by the practice of prompting Artificial Intelligence to give us output that suits our purpose. The form, content and specificity of the question can be very important. Also critical is whether the prompt should be a question, a request or a command.

The Question Formulation Technique (QFT)™

This is a simple step-by-step, rigorous process that facilitates the asking of many questions. The process includes the following steps:

- Question Focus (QFocus)
- The Rules for Producing Questions
- Producing Questions
- Categorizing Questions
- Prioritizing Questions
- Next Steps
- Reflection

1. The Question Focus (QFocus) – A stimulus; a springboard you will use to ask questions. The QFocus can be a topic, image, phrase or situation that will serve as the "focus" for generating questions. An effective QFocus should be clear, should provoke and stimulate new lines of thinking and should not be a question.

2. The Rules for Producing Questions – Each of the four rules supports a behavior that facilitates effective question formulation.

- Ask as many questions as you can

- Do not stop to discuss, judge, or answer any questions
- Write down every question exactly as it is stated
- Change any statement into a question

The first step for producing questions is to review the rules and name potential challenges in following them.

The rules can be difficult to follow at times because you are being asked to work in a way that might be new or different from what you are accustomed to. The goal here is to create awareness of the difficulties and help you abide by the rules as you work on producing questions.

3. Produce Questions – You will use the Question Focus (QFocus) to formulate as many questions as you can. Ask all kinds of questions about the topic, phrase, image, situation, etc. presented. Please make sure to follow the rules.

This part of the process allows you to think freely without having to worry about the quality of the questions you are asking.

4. Improving the Questions – Once you have a list of questions, the next step is to learn about two different types of questions you might have on your list: *closed-ended questions* – questions that can be answered with a "yes" or "no" or with one word – and *open-ended questions* – questions that require an explanation. This part of the process develops as follows:

1. First, please review your list and identify the closed-ended questions with a "C" and the open-ended with an "O."
2. Second, think about and name the advantages and disadvantages of asking each type of question. You will see that there is value in asking both types of questions.

3. Third, practice changing questions from one type to another. Changing the questions will help you learn how to edit your questions to meet your purpose.

5. Prioritizing Questions – You might have a lot of questions on your list. It will be easier to work with the questions if some priorities are established. You will now choose three questions based on actions you want to take. For example, three most important questions, three questions you would like to address first, three questions you want to explore further, etc.

After choosing the priority questions, your next step is to name a rationale for choosing.

As a last step in prioritizing, please pay attention to the numbers of your priority questions. Are your priority questions at the beginning, in the middle, or at the end?

6. Next Steps – Your questions can now be put into action. You might already have criteria on what to do with the questions. For example, you may use the questions to do research, develop a project, use the questions as a guide, etc.

7. Reflection – This is the last step in the process. It is now time to reflect on the work you have done: what you have learned and how you can use it. The reflection helps internalize the process, its value and how to apply it further.[9]

In businesses that thrive on innovation and want to cut through the constant posturing of meetings filled with only declarations, this process that helps the team develop better focus through asking the right questions could prove quite valuable. In addition, one may want to support efforts to expand this kind of emphasis on questioning in the world's educational systems as a means of promoting healthy dialogue in business.

Fortunately, there is a lot of emphasis in business development now on asking questions and listening to answers, but what if we don't know how to ask the right questions? One could wonder if an education system that teaches to test, rather than stimulating and responding to individual inquisitive minds, has prepared students to know how to ever question outside the box.

If business is inheriting people who have not been taught to question appropriately, or to practice inquisitive or critical thinking, companies are forced to have leadership that thinks for employees. We all could cite examples that would confirm that if you think <u>for</u> people, they will generally let you. The net result is a loss of important knowledge and input that can create dynamic teamwork, innovation and success so vital for a competitive business world. Generally, in the current business environment twenty people thinking is a stronger team than two people thinking and the rest undertaking thoughtless activity.

Here are nine additional pointers for leadership communication in meetings that encourage critical and creative thinking:

- Ask open-ended, strategic questions to stimulate thinking.
- Signal that questioning is okay.
- Attempt to answer and to ask others to answer when questions are asked.
- Take time to listen to the answers.
- Think of what's behind the questions and follow up with probing questions.
- Pose challenges as questions.
- Don't discount questions, whatever their source.
- Give the questioners encouragement by bringing results.
- Acknowledge the importance and acceptance of inquiry.

Business people may not be able to immediately impact an education system that suppresses inquiry, but we can run our companies in a way that underscores the importance of engaged thinking at all levels of the organization.

The measure of our success in this endeavor will determine the level at which we are able to create and sustain learning organizations. In a world of fast-moving technology and innovation, it is the learning individuals and learning organizations that will inherit the future.

TWELVE

Transparency

One of the more challenging questions in business communication is, "How much transparency should an organization have?" How much and what information should be public, internal or limited-distribution internal? It's a difficult decision because it gets to the heart of the authenticity, truth and trust discussed in previous chapters. How can one be authentic if not trusted, and how much can one be trusted when there are too many secrets?

A friend was struggling with this when she explained recently that she and her spouse hadn't been sure how much of the family finances to discuss with their college-aged son. She said they were required to make quite an effort and cut lots of financial corners to be able to afford his sizable college tuition. "I just didn't want him to worry," she said, "I was afraid it would distract him from his studies."

Months into the son's freshman year, it was apparent that too many parties were cutting into his study time. "We wondered at that point," she explained, "if being more transparent with him about the effort we were making would have made a difference in his dedication to studying."

I found a similar struggle while visiting with the CEO of a startup biotech business. All of the lab scientists in the small company were hard at work being innovative. The CEO was torn between keeping them up to date on all of the difficulties that existed with making sure the company was continually financed by investors, and allowing employees to be unaware and secure so they could keep inventing. "I don't want them to find themselves looking for work on short notice because I can't come up with money," he said.

At the same time, he knew he was quite confident and a lot more knowledgeable about the potential investors and the future than he could ever explain to his employees. He had to balance the guilt of not being transparent against the consequences of losing people who became insecure, even though he knew the company was on the verge of a financial breakthrough. Was it his job to insulate the scientists or to have them proceed, aware of the potential outcomes?

The business leader faced with such a difficult decision would do well to be reminded that secrecy is a two-way street. In that laboratory, there may have been scientists with their own knowledge of problems who were reluctant to share that information with the CEO because it might impact his ability to raise money. (in fact that was exactly the case. Everybody thought they were protecting everybody else.) This is why we would make a point that transparency with appropriateness and discretion should be preferred. Discretion can certainly be an important factor as part of the art of leadership, and discretion is part of what makes leadership an art.

Deadly Error in Leadership Communication

In one of the most troubling examples of dangers arising from a lack of transparency, recent investigations uncovered a hospital's shortcomings that were putting the lives of tens of thousands of newborn infants at risk.

In 2013, an article in the *Milwaukee Journal Sentinel* newspaper reported the results of a study of the records of three million newborns in the United States with shocking details of infant deaths. The newspaper reported hospitals were delaying life-saving newborn blood screening tests and risking the health and lives of tens of thousands of babies. Newborns are supposed to be screened before they leave the hospital. The Centers for Disease Control positions it this way:

> All babies are screened, even if they look healthy, because some medical conditions cannot be seen by just looking at the baby. Finding these conditions soon after birth can help prevent some serious problems, such as brain damage, organ damage and even death.
>
> For example, a test for phenylketonuria (PKU) checks if the baby's body can process phenylalanine. Phenylalanine is found in many protein-rich foods and some sweeteners and can build up in the blood and tissues of a baby with PKU, resulting in brain damage. This can be prevented if a baby with PKU is put on a special diet early. Babies are also tested for hypothyroidism, which means that their bodies do not make enough thyroid hormone. Babies with hypothyroidism can take medication with the hormone to avoid the slowed growth and brain damage that can happen if their hypothyroidism is not treated.[1]

Some babies not properly screened could have a condition in which their own mother's milk is literally poison to them. The *Journal Sentinel* reporters found instances where up to 29% of newborn blood samples in one state didn't reach the lab until five days or more after the birth. Babies actually died as a result of a failure of the system to make sure screening took place in a timely fashion.

The *Journal Sentinel*, in its award-winning series of articles, reported that in some instances, hospitals were cutting costs and reducing trouble by saving the tests until the end of the week, then turning them all in at once. Some babies weren't tested. Many tests were mishandled.

The public outrage after the focus of attention resulted in quick action on the part of many of the hospitals in the country.

From an organizational communication standpoint, allowing this crisis to occur was a monumental failure of leaders who should have been taking responsibility. The ineptitude displayed in this story speaks volumes about the lack of caring, professionalism, listening and transparency in many of the organizations where the problems occurred. Somewhere, there had to have been employees who knew the approach being taken was a mistake. Among the hundreds of thousands of persons involved in newborn care, many most certainly should have known of the risks involved in the delay of screening.

One can surmise that those people either didn't speak up for lack of interest or threat of being intimidated, or they simply thought it would do no good. As a result, babies died, and some had developmental problems and crippling illnesses because of the error being treated with such secrecy.

Just the simple instigation of a culture of openness and the willingness on the part of leadership to hear and understand in context, even negative or critical input, could have spared an incalculable measure of pain and grief for the children and families impacted. This was not an organizational failure. It was a failure on a massive scale of individuals in leadership who either didn't know better, or were too detached or intimidated to challenge flawed practices.

Give Transparency to Get Transparency

Business dealings are often time-sensitive, carry sensitivities of competitive secrets, or have some level of ambiguity that must be addressed before being made general knowledge. At the same time, one can't expect transparency and an open conduit of information if that openness is perceived as being one-sided and going in only one direction.

In this balance, it's preferable to lean toward the policy of transparency. This doesn't mean telling everyone every detail you know. It means having the integrity and authenticity to avoid being deceptive. It means being willing to weigh carefully the motivation and impacts of withholding information.

In dealing with crisis communication, I have often seen huge problems suddenly appear because leaders refused to be forthcoming about hints of risks along the way. Those risks often arise from a situation in which trouble is building over time, with people deep in the organization stuffing it down, hiding or ignoring signs. Those people either thought top management didn't want to hear about it, or they feared consequences if they revealed the truth.

Nothing is more threatening to a top-level executive than to be kept isolated from the facts of the operation. The philosophy of "What I don't know won't hurt me" or the idea that "I can't be accused of non-compliance if I didn't know it was happening" represents a leadership style that is flirting with disaster.

University leaders across the United States were in the early two thousands stricken with a stark reality of the need for more transparency in their operations. The U.S. Department of Education's Office for Civil Rights (OCR) enforces Title IX of the Education Amendments of 1972. Title IX stated that:

> No person in the United States shall, on the basis of sex, be excluded from participation in, be denied the benefits of, or be subjected to discrimination under any education program or activity receiving Federal financial assistance.

Title IX supposedly applies to institutions that receive federal financial assistance from the Department of Education, including state and local educational agencies and universities. The Office for Civil Rights at one point undertook an investigation of specific universities' handling of sexual assault cases, viewing this as one of the most egregious of the civil rights violations on campus. It is anybody's guess what the future of this enforcement may be, given the current political climate.

For a time, the investigations created quite a shock in the ivory towers of higher education. They found in some institutions a look-the-other-way approach when fraternities or sports teams were involved in rape investigations.

The academic leaders were caught between the heavy influence of big donors, the substantial income from sports, the extreme sensitivity of the subject matter for institutional reputation, and the potential for both the alleged victims and the accused perpetrators to sue universities claiming these matters were mishandled.[2]

The discovery of a traditional blocking of the flow of vital information about sexual assault that had taken place throughout large, often stodgy university management systems has come as quite a shock to some of the institutions investigated by the Office of Civil Rights.

The investigations and revelations were a response to years of institutional practices that brushed over and obscured facts of sexual assault on campus. The extent of psychological trauma to young victims may never be known. A culture of transparency could have prevented a lot of suffering.

Since the first writing of this book, an unraveling of the Department of Education has taken place, along with a rather dramatic revision of the governmental approach to campus sexual assault. Some may argue that the "see something, say something" approach had gone too far, with professors becoming so inhibited that they feared having any interaction with students. The entire matter of whose civil rights are being protected and how is now a bit of a quagmire. Transparency may no longer be the standard.

Bury Your Head (and we still see parts of you)

A corporate culture of clandestine, deceptive dialogue fosters a system fraught with risks. Especially as a corporate officer, what a person doesn't know can hurt them. There is an expectation that an executive should know certain information in the exercise of appropriate diligence of operation.

In interpreting the Responsible Corporate Officer Doctrine, the courts have held some corporate officers responsible for misconduct, even when they weren't aware of the specifics of the violation. It is established that corporate stakeholders have a right to expect that persons in an official position of authority protect their interests. While enforcement of much of this doctrine has been made to apply to the pharmaceutical and medical device industries, the rules are still there for any executive to ponder.[3]

The doctrine can apply when the circumstance meets three standards:

i. that "the prohibited act took place somewhere within the company"
ii. "the defendant's position within the company was one that gave him or her responsibility and

authority either to prevent the violation or correct it"

iii. that he or she did not do so.[4]

Transparency Even in a Crisis?

Transparency before a crisis could prevent the crisis. It's also true that in the middle of a crisis, transparency can be a valuable asset for resolution.

An older movie called *China Syndrome* is the story of the meltdown of a nuclear plant. In that movie, what we would refer to today as a whistleblower has taken over the control room of the plant. In one scene, you see the president of the company in a room overlooking the control room. He is talking to a subdued-looking PR person.

The whistleblower, who is now in charge of the plant control room, has asked to see the media. In the scene, the president says to the PR person, "Well, at least we can buy some time; it will take the press at least an hour to get here." To this the rather mousy-looking PR person responds, "...wouldn't count on that." The president then sternly says, "Look, I am counting on you to take care of the god damn press. Now you do your job, and I'll do mine."

In a subsequent scene, the viewer sees the media arrive like an army at the gate of the plant. The same reticent PR person is saying, "We don't have anything to say right now, if you gentlemen could just be patient."

That scene demonstrates the idea of response to crisis that is held by some in management. Many may say this would not be their own response, but when the chips are down, management begins to migrate toward this head-in-the-sand kind of position.

And the position is: "Look, the crisis has happened, we need to have the techies and the administrative people protected so they can take care of the situation." This seems to make sense in the minds of those who believe the crisis is all mechanical or administrative. They may think: "If we can take care of the mechanical and administrative crisis and PR can just keep the public out of our hair while we do that, everything will be fine."

There can sometimes be a mindset in corporate management and among technically-minded individuals that maybe delay and trickery is what the communication side of things is all about. Handling both internal and external communicating is sometimes viewed as a kind of touchy-feely thing, sort of an instinct one has when they are "good with people." It is too often seen by some in management as simply "good BS skills."

Thirty years ago, reporters and employees were a little less aggressive. They still wanted their stories, but they were also more respectful of certain lines that were not to be crossed. In that era, corporations could say "no comment" in the face of a crisis, and that would suffice until they said something else.

Even police, firefighters, competitors and regulators were willing to be only quietly aggressive or assertive in getting another story out when the corporation was trying to get its story put together and hold the line for a while. After all, it was a crisis, and reporters could all patiently wait to get the real story. Everybody trusted and relied on the reporters, corporate spokespersons, regulators, etc. a little more in those days.

Now we all know there is an expectation for solutions to arrive at our door at about the same time as problems. So if a problem arises, various stakeholders expect to know almost instantly what the solution will be. This is a time when a reporter, the public and even an organization's employees can hear simultaneously that there has been a small leak of hydrofluoric acid, for example, at a site. In a short period of time, tapping into all the computer databases available to the public, a person can become a self-perceived hydrofluoric acid expert.

One can suddenly know all the damning possibilities that come with that particular chemical. So that person can show up at a news conference, maybe knowing more about hydrofluoric acid than a company spokesperson does.

Now with social media and hundreds of Creators believing they run a news source, the authorities at the scene may not have the first (or the last word). By the time corporate spokespersons decide to speak, memes may have been put in place, and misinformation based on observation, opposition, or competition has become so convincing that the corporate message is reduced to "just another voice."

There is a new wave of belief that numerous parties are stakeholders in what an organization does. Corporations are woven into the fabric of the community in such a way that the various agencies and organizations are requesting and sometimes demanding high levels of partnering in the decisions made and the actions taken by a company. This includes the public interposing access to even the decision-making process. So, the idea of "at least it will take the media an hour to get here," and the attitude of "you take care of the god damn press, I am going to run the crisis," doesn't work anymore, if it ever did.

So, What Does Work?

What works is having a culture of transparency that allows one to immediately establish an open, responsive, credible communication with stakeholders. And this is not just talking about the media. Stakeholders in a corporation or organization may include employees, legislators, regulators and the various publics out in the community.

One of the well-known examples of organizational public relations failure was the Three Mile Island nuclear plant accident in 1979. There was a twelve-hour blackout on information. This, while there was an enormous amount of speculation in just how widespread the impacts of a "nuclear meltdown" might be felt.

Seven years later, businesses still had a lot to learn about transparency in a crisis. On January 28, 1986, the United States National Aeronautics and Space Administration's spacecraft Challenger exploded after liftoff. There was a public information blackout from NASA for over half a day. The blackout contributed heavily to the initial bad press the agency received.

Following an initial announcement, there was about a six-month blackout of substantive news. The lack of immediacy ultimately resulted in NASA getting some pretty tough media and public reception for messaging on the incident.

Seventeen years later, NASA lost another spacecraft. On February 1, 2003, the space shuttle Columbia blew apart, killing seven astronauts. As a result of previous mistakes, the agency had learned something about transparency.

In this instance, there was broad recognition in the media, Congress and the public that, compared to the Challenger incident, the agency had excelled in truthfulness, transparency, promptness of response, choice and availability of spokespersons, and expressions of compassion.[5]

Another comparison example is the Catholic Church and the crisis in priestly sexual morality. It was the kind of crisis that can foment over time and sneak up on an organization. Leaders might not recognize a slow-growing crisis until it unfolds, and at some point along the way, someone says, "Gee, this looks like a crisis for the whole organization." This may come after the response is too late or inappropriate.

Transparency has to work through the culture. Sudden and surprise transparency can sometimes backfire. There were some challenging things that went on in the early years in the US Department of Energy. Hair-raising stories eventually surfaced about radioactive materials used in medical tests and about other careless activities.

In 1989, incoming new United States Department of Energy Secretary Admiral James D. Watkins took office, promising a "new culture of accountability at the Department of Energy." He invited the Labor Department's Occupational Safety and Health Administration (OSHA) into DOE plant operations for the first time. The department sent out "Tiger Teams" charged with uncovering problems and ultimately made some very revealing announcements.[6]

What Admiral Watkins didn't do was work that process of transparency down through the organization before he made the revelation of all the problems. Within the DOE operational organization, some people felt like they had been sold out. They had been abiding for years by a policy that was necessarily much less open, much more clandestine than the one Watkins instituted. They had also heroically and secretly won the nuclear arms race, despite poisoning a few people along the way. Now the Secretary was making announcements that made the department look good for its new transparency, but often reflected poorly on the older ank and file.

So one just doesn't decide one day: "Oh, let's be transparent today." It's something that has to be integrated into the corporate environment. In that instance, when a crisis happens, it's easier to have transparency at the top and through the ranks. Then the people in the ranks don't feel betrayed. It may seem tough to make a switch to transparency in advance of a crisis, but if one has training and has parameters for this openness to make it credible, the potential for rewarding interaction is heightened. The best approach is to build a culture of transparency into a team initially and at every stage of a project.

THIRTEEN

Communicating Risks

Most leaders must deal with some manifestation of risks in their profession. This can be risks for the business, for clients, employees and, sometimes, the public. Preventing or properly containing/managing risks is integral for good business.

An ability to recognize, identify, acknowledge and appropriately communicate risks is crucial to effective management.

A U.S. government publication quotes financial analysts as suggesting that up to seventy percent of an organization's value is in intangibles such as goodwill that are threatened when risk communication is not handled properly.

No matter what industry you work in, there are likely regulations requiring appropriate communication of risks, and consequences for not doing so. "Right to know" obligations can require that employees and other stakeholders be informed of various risks and consequences.

Risk messages can be among the greatest communication challenges because they are particularly difficult to construct in a way that is accurate, clear, motivational for response and not misleading or self-serving.

In the United States, we can look to the *U.S. Food and*

Drug Administration (FDA) as an example. That agency regulates industries that account for up to twenty percent of the U.S. economy. The agency is in the business of identifying and mitigating risks.

This author has listened to hundreds of hours of witnesses for FDA hearings describe, debate, dissect and opine on details of risks of various drugs and products and the potential methods of addressing those risks. These are matters of constant review and debate, and there are no flawless, surefire formulas. Despite the fact that medical/device/product approvals can often come only after weigh-in from the most informed experts around the world, the agency often comes under criticism for not doing enough to control risks.

A publication from the FDA entitled "Communicating Risks and Benefits: An Evidence-Based User's Guide," spells out the measurements for adequacy of a risk communication, saying it is adequate if:

- It contains the information needed for effective decision-making
- Users can access that information, and users can comprehend what they access
- It contains any information that might affect a significant fraction of users' choices
- It puts most users within X degrees of separation of the needed information, given their normal search patterns.
- Most users can extract enough information to make sound choices[1]

Forthcoming, candid, and accurate identification of a risk can be crucial for generating an appropriate response. Obfuscation or ignoring of a risk can compound the anxiety experienced as it evolves. Effective risk communication reduces misunderstandings and overreactions to risks and is designed to prompt appropriate responses and remedies. It presents in proper context and with plain language the following elements for the risk:

- Identification
- Characterization
- Bounding
- Knowledge for aversion methods
- Timing
- Understanding of personalization
- Explanation of potential consequences
- Approaches to address the consequences
- Approach(es) to remedy the risk at its source
- Method(s) or measurements for recognition of risk termination or signs of reduction

Also helpful, but not always possible, is the inclusion of a method for the originator of a risk communication message to evaluate the effectiveness of that effort in order to retune the message if needed.

Identify the Risk

Specific and accurate Identification and attribution of the source of a risk is critical to giving a proper perspective.

A risk communication is set apart in that it is not a spin or a public relations announcement. Identification of the risk(s) should be made straightforwardly and candidly without adornment.

Risk identification should be to the point and as specific as one can appropriately make it. Don't play games. Don't be tricky; It will backfire later.

What one wants to avoid is opining on some detailed characterization and contextualization of a risk to try to "set the stage" before the actual risk is clearly identified. All of us have seen news conferences where politicians extol the "wonderful work" of a response team for thirty minutes before a crisis or the risk is detailed. It builds resentment.

Remember, your ownership of the right to identify and characterize a risk is now short-lived in our era of internet searches. Increasingly, risk messages do not occur in a vacuum. Those revealing crisis or breaking news of risks can often find a room full of reporters who may believe they already know as much about the subject as the speaker. Employees may have already passed around information on a risk themselves and "researched" (done an internet search of) details before anything to unfold.

All of the elements of risk communication described in our bullet list above will probably be detailed for the listener by some internet source (or friend with a digital device) and may be totally at odds with your message. You primarily have one shot early. Make sure it is early and make it count. It may be the only or cleanest shot you will get at making sure you believe the message is accurate.

Characterize (Frame) the Risk

Characterization of the risk should be done with appropriate and candid framing. (See the chapter [9] on framing and scaffolding.)

Framing of a risk in context becomes extremely important but should not be done in a way that obscures or improperly minimizes the risk(s).

Providing a simple, plain language perspective on the nature of and situation with the risk generally has more (we might say) "stickability" if it is short, pointed and candid. This can be followed immediately by bounding.

Getting people to change behavior or alter attitudes based on risk can be a daunting task. The framing of a risk message is critical to that message being heard and embraced.

In order to be taken seriously, risk messages should be clear, logical and make sense. The book Remove Child Before Folding offers collection of risk admonitions that can border on the ridiculous. One for a cooking pot, for example, warns that "Ovenware will get hot when used in oven."[2]

Avoid spinning the characterization of the risk. This can sometimes be a subtle attempt to present details in a self-serving way that obscures understanding.

One most famous example of this appears in a 1986 *Washington Post* story about the Soviet's positioning of the Chernobyl nuclear explosion incident. The simple truth was that the disaster had the potential to result in 35,000 to 45,000 cancer deaths in the (then) Soviet Union and that as many as 90,000 people could be affected by the explosion. The Soviets represented that this would be "less than ,05 percent in relation to the death rate due to spontaneously occurring cancer."

As it turned out, that .05 percent equaled 35,000 to 45,000 people, but it was a much different sounding message that could be expected to elicit a quite different perception of risk in most people. It was a tricky way to obscure the risk. The *Washington Post* article was entitled, "Chernobyl Report Surprisingly Detailed but Avoids Painful Truths, Experts Say."[3]

Spinny manipulation to underplay risks can backfire with an outcome of eroding trust from the audience, when trust may be needed most.

Communicators generally cannot assume that everyone reacts the same to risk or weighs the message with the same set of expectations or values. An example that this author has used in several publications involves attitudes toward gambling. It's a good example because it demonstrates that we all are built differently in our measure of risk acceptability.

Individuals tend to have a variation in the way we respond to taking risks or addressing high stakes. Some people tend to approach assessing the stakes of a situation based on what could be lost, while others are more likely to base their assessment on what can be gained.

Examined under the label "Prospect Theory," or "Decision Making Under Risk," this idea is that the outcome of risk assessment may depend heavily on a person's orientation to seek gaining something or avoid losing.

Consider people in a casino when a slot machine has a mediocre pay-off. Some will take their winnings and consider themselves lucky, others will continue to play the same slot machine, thinking the interim payoff is leading to the big hit.

Scientists now believe that each of these motivations in seeking the win or avoiding the loss involves different parts and functions of the brain in dealing with risk. This means one can't just look at any given person and predict what risk will mean to them.

There is also research that suggests these risk avoidance or risk defiance reactions may be different for men and women. Thus, different people may be assessing your risk messaging, even with different parts of their brains. This is depending on how they react to risks in general.

It is also true that many circumstances in which we find ourselves may include the potential for both loss and gain, thus the popularity of presenting risk/benefit messaging.[4]

How one seeks to avoid loss and how one anticipates gain come into play in a sometimes complicated intertwining of emotions. This suggest the need to include both how to implement the active steps to success the potential end result of loss or a gain.

Bound (or Fence) the Risk

It is extremely important in bringing perspective and conceptualization to provide bounds for the risk(s).

This means making a proper representation of what the area, circumstance, reach, and/or area of potential impact of the risk happens to be. Put a fence around it.

For example, watch the television weather alerts and a tornado warning. Generally, the radar and various computer programs will show the area of the report, the populated places at potential risk, the expected trajectory and the location(s) of the most immediate threat. There is no reason for people in the whole state to cover themselves up with a mattress in the bathtub. What this usually does, however, is to identify the areas of most threatening risk and describe appropriate measures that should be taken in those areas. This focuses on the nature of the expediency.

There is not much more disturbing to the public than an ill-defined, unbounded risk.

Bounding can set up the level of need for, and the details for appropriate mitigation.

An example of unwanted ambiguity might be an announcement that "water is deadly." Yep. If you are in enough of it, under the right circumstances, you might need to swim! If you don't get enough of it, you could die of dehydration. It is a matter of proper identification, context and bounding for risks associated with water.

One big advantage of your message bounding of a risk is that it allows one to anticipate an increase in the likelihood of urgency and potential for response in relation to the relative urgency and proximity of the risk.

One of the biggest mistakes people make in risk communication is inadequately bounding risks in communicating them. Sometimes, it is impossible, but often not.

Lawyers may have reason to push back on this, but they also have to weigh the end-run, big picture liability and objectives in having to choose between candid/effective, and "safe," but obscure communication. It can also be important to consider there may be differences in liability when communicating about risk, addressing a crisis, or doing both at the same time. Crisis communication is a different subject that encompasses risk messaging.

A publication from the National Research Council described the dilemma in the public announcement of an accident this way:

> "Communication and Public Relations experts usually advise making available everything that is known about the accident as quickly as possible, in terms that laypeople can readily understand. Legal advice is almost always the opposite: give out as little information as possible. so as to avoid providing ammunition for use in court. ...The final message probably involves a compromise between these objectives."[5]

In an environment where there are increasingly multiple sources vying for attention in the revelation of risks and people instantly start to search through online details, it is important to give weight to the potential for loss of trust and credibility in being stingy with detail. One can thus lose the positioning as the primary source for information and any ability to control the narrative.

We can say here that (at the time of this writing) we are at a place when using Large Language Model (LLM) prompted output to write a risk message can be either too flowery and spinny, or too insensitive to all of the subtleties we have just discussed to be used without a great deal of specificity in the prompt or heavy editing of the outcome.

If you use an LLM, be careful yo carefully review and tune

the message. Put a fence around (bound) the description of risk with your message when it is appropriate and you can. It takes some strategic decision making.

Provide Timing Context

What is the time factor for a risk? What is the expectation for it to persist, get worse or to play-out over time? Sometimes this can be highly predictable, at other times, highly uncertain. It may be that the best that one can do in an ambiguous situation is to commit to reassessment and updates.

For a fun exercise on this subject, one might watch the TV series "The Pitt" created by R. Scott Gemmill and appearing on *Max*. Set in a hospital emergency room, it is a constant and ingenious rollout of risk messaging and receiver perceptions. There are examples of various expertise in messaging and good or bad consequences. The show is a rapid-fire delivery of examples of explaining risks. This is done under stress, often with immediate response.

"The Pitt" is heralded for its realism and might be considered by the student of communication as a drone view of risk messaging in a pressure cooker. This is all occurring under constant insistence from the hospital administration to boost the "patient satisfaction" rating.

Spell Out Aversion Methods

Effective risk communication provides the information necessary for the recipient of the message to understand, avoid, diminish and/or eliminate the risk. In other words, it contains the information needed for effective decision-making. This assumes the risk origination and characterization can be identified and understood? Can it be avoided? Can it be diminished? Can it be eliminated? These factors are the big challenge for any spokesperson who may be tempted to minimize or obscure detailing of a risk.

Again, there is a need to strike a balance. Will too much detail generate fear, dramatization and overreaction? Will insufficient detail mean there is not enough information to guide reaction? There may very well be liability on both sides of the equation.

This can get complicated. In some instances, addressing one risk means the introduction of new/different risks presented by the resolution. This is common, for example, in medicine. A primary challenge there for balancing risk and benefit in being able to identify and control the risk of the remedies.

The goals can be to identify the method(s) for resolving the risk, ability to recognize when it has been resolved, and may need to include proper perspective on the risk of the remedy and proper administration nd monitoring of that.

An FDA publication emphasizes a challenge that people in leadership often assume or take for granted that just because they know something, others know it too.

"People exaggerate how well they understand others' perspectives. This general tendency, perhaps familiar to most people in their everyday communication has many expressions. Here is how an FDA document on risks explained it:

> "People exaggerate how much of their knowledge is shared by others. As a result, they fail to say important things, expecting others to know them already. Thus, a physician might assume that patients know that they will be tired long after a surgery; salespeople might assume that customers know that they will be hot (or itchy) wearing a new fabric; grocers may assume that people know that bar codes do not guarantee that a food is traceable to its source, in case of an outbreak. Without knowing what people know already,

communicators cannot know which outcomes to include in their messages."[6]

This idea is now confounded by Artificial Intelligence and the fact that people may now know instantly as much or more than than an organizational spokesperson knows about an issue. It is also complicated by the fact that this awareness may run totally contrary to what the company team assumed the recipients would know about details of a risk. Large Language Models cannot be assumed to be always correct in their output about highly technical issues.

Bring It Home

Risks are not the same for everyone. All of us have seen television news announcers say something like, "we will report on the impacts to your wallet from prices climbing at the local grocery store, right after this message." Good journalism schools teach students to personalize messages, or "bring it home" to the listener by talking about how the individual is impacted. The closer to home a risk tends to be, the more one pays attention and the greater the likelihood of an appropriate response to the risk.

As an example, we might look at an announcement that "criminals are targeting gym members for car theft." That story is of less interest if one is not a gym member. If the message is "Car thieves are striking at Happy Barbell gyms across the country," It becomes more critical for members of the Happy Barbell gym chain. If the story names your local gym and says that thieves are stealing cars at gyms where members generally hang their car keys on a peg when they walk in, the listener who hangs their car keys on a peg at that specific local Happy Barbell become quite interested and quickly understand how to respond to the threat.

Taking it a step further, one could say that the news story includes that on February 2nd the gym management removed all of the car key pegboards from the gym to reduce the threat after they were able to document the thefts on video and help police arrest the culprits.

Now, we know the risk, the setting, methods and some of the origin of the risk, we also know about the introduction of a possible remedy and the timing of that.

We can suggest that appropriate response to risks is more compelling when the consequences are understood and when they are brought closer to home.

We have suggested in this chapter that individuals understand and respond to consequences differently. (Someone with a faulty car they want to dump night be rushing up to the local Joyful Barbell to hang their keys on a peg.)

It is also true that consequences are sometimes weighed against the cost of remedy. Many may have seen a video of the joke by Present Lyndon Johnson about the older man whose doctor warned him that if he didn't quit drinking so much, he would lose his hearing.

In the joke, the man responds that he may not cut the drinking because, "I like what I drink so much better than what I hear."

Of course, the key message here is that risk communicators must know and respond to the audience and what motivates the individuals. Given that potential that responders are not the same, the message may need to take several forms for remedies, mitigation or resolution to be embraced and implemented by the recipients.

Some may be more motivated by the potential for gain than the potential for loss. Some may be so off-put by the cost to them of the remedy that they just decide to accept the risk. Legal constraints may also impact the message and the measure by which you as a spokesperson can candidly be the source of detail.

We also know that there may be multiple sources where those at potential risk may run to for information. Those sources could shed a totally different light on the message you are trying to send. The wise communicator will have made that online search ahead of time and know what will be found alternatively by those who decide to seek more information elsewhere.

Risk communication is not an off-the-cuff endeavor and may need to involve a lot of strategic planning. Done properly, it can inform, equip and empower the potential for risk resolution or mitigation.

PART IV
Bringing it all together

FOURTEEN

Authenticity

> Be yourself. Everyone else is already taken. – Oscar Wilde

> The privilege of a lifetime is to become who you truly are. – C.G. Jung

One of the most important statements one can make about human interaction is that communication is not a performance. The most powerful rule for effective communication is authenticity.

If one thinks of authenticity as something being exactly what it is, or someone being exactly who they are, it could be hard to think of a situation in which there wouldn't be authenticity, in which there wouldn't be adherence to reality, right? Not exactly.

Unfortunately, people have experiences out of which they develop something other than authenticity and that's where the big problem arises for communicating.

How can that happen? Well, it certainly can happen as

we're growing up. It can develop starting in infancy. William and Martha Sears in their online resource "Ask Doctor Sears," Talk about what they describe as "The Disconnected Infant.":

> A baby who is dutifully scheduled, left to cry it out and whose well-meaning parents fall prey to the fear-of-spoiling advice, learns early that the caregiving world is not responsive to his needs. He learns to stop asking. This baby learns to ignore his feelings at an early age. He learns neither to identify nor to express them. On the surface, this little person is a "good" baby; he doesn't bother anybody. He adjusts to the inflexible schedule, sleeps through the night and is convenient to have around. This "good" baby, seemingly so "well-disciplined," is at risk for becoming a withdrawn child and an internally angry, depressed adult.[1]

This early experience sets in motion an inauthenticity in individual interaction, which, unfortunately, is just compounded when children interact with larger groups.

From the time we were children, many of us had instances when we were encouraged to perform. These were our first experiences of being asked to communicate to a group of people. This may have been aunts, uncles, family members, or friends. In the company of these family/friends, we were brought into a room (maybe at the age of three, four, or five years old) and asked to perform a poem or sing a little song. It might have been "I'm A Little Teapot" or maybe "Itsy Bitsy Spider," but most of the time when we were asked to communicate with more than three people at a time, it was a performance.

It was not a dialogue, not an interaction; it was a performance, sometimes with very contrived gestures. It was emphasized to us that we were there to perform, show how cute, or how smart we were. Some of us took to it better than others, and some had a better experience at this than others.

Many adults fear public presentations. There is a prevalence of performance anxiety associated with speaking to groups of people. We can solve that in part with this admonition: Decide you won't perform.

In varying degrees, we may all be encountering the temptation to become only partially invested in our interactions by being very good at acting and performing.

Avoid Performing Your Presence

One of the greatest impediments for effective presentation and communicating is the idea of performance. One does not perform being an effective witness, nor making a media statement nor delivering an announcement to employees. A performance approach to presenting can't contain the subtle nonverbals and the authentic tone of sincerity that actual, two-way human dialogue provides.

All that we have said in this book about caring, empathy, being invested, knowing and understanding your audience and being comfortable with your content come together in making communication impactful, powerful, influential and persuasive in a much more valuable way than performance ever can. What we might call *"Engaged Interaction"* pushes through messages on almost every channel of brain function in a way that prompts engagement on the part of the receiver.

Unfortunately, performance interaction is so common and expected that it can suffice in many cases in business. It will do. As a mark of mediocrity, quick and dirty dispatch and shallow, disconnected discourse, being a performer can certainly get one by in today's business activities. It pales, however, as a means for excellence and success in communicating.

Eventually, shallow performing will play out with the experience of people not paying attention, discounting what you say, or simply disconnecting from any thought of being motivated by your comments.

Here are some guidelines for **Engaged Interaction:**

- Be fully present – bring all of you and your mental capacity to the table.
- Make eye contact.
- Tap some passion in yourself.
- Invest your body by having natural movement, facial expression and gestures.
- Expect and acknowledge the presence of others and pleasantly challenge mental absenteeism by fully engaging the audience. Get closer, involve the audience.
- Do your homework to make sure what you're saying has some meaning.
- Understand and acknowledge the audience's connection with the information.
- Deliver some value for your audience and make sure they know what that value is.
- Be comfortable with your own presence and identity.
- If you are going to use AI to prepare any of your material and remarks, make sure you have edited the output to personalize it to your preferences and style.

One could write untold chapters on communication style. One could suggest where to put your hands, how long to hold eye contact, what to do with your voice, but all of that can come into place quite nicely when a speaker is fully informed, fully invested and fully engaged with an audience.

You're not Judy Garland, for goodness sake. Quit performing.

FIFTEEN

Just a Face on Video

What image do you convey on camera?

There is much that can now be gained (or lost) by how one comes across in virtual meetings. Working by video has become increasingly important in all our lives. Most of us have given attention to our appearance at the office. It is just as important to have a professional look, demeanor and environment online when we want to be respected in business. These are pointers for simply showing up with a good presence on camera.

Be Human

The first goal here is to be yourself. Be human. Increasingly, online presence is being provided by deep fake or text-to-speech Artificial Intelligence entities that can sound very lifelike. This is the cutting edge of an era that will soon see all kinds of communication outlets filled with these non-human, but quite realistic speakers.

If your business *frowns* on a human touch with observations, expressions, side comments, and signs of authentic people presence, those ideas need to be reviewed. For online meetings to be real and most productive, one needs to encourage some of the same kind of human interaction that happens in personal encounters.

That's not to say to waste time. As noted in other sections of this book, being fully present with all that entails is crucial for maintaining healthy business relationships. This is the element AI communicators can't (yet) bring to interactions. The guidelines here help to maximize personhood in online attendance and, perhaps, delay the day when automation and data exchange take over the business meeting.

Camera Placement

This is key to human engagement. The camera should be at, or slightly above, eye level. You may need a tripod, a box, or a stack of books to accomplish this. Looking down at the camera distorts your face and the lighting. It can make your hair frame your face poorly. This is not a vantage point anyone (but pets and children) normally encounters in person-to-person contact.

Having a camera look up at you also deepens below-the-eye shadows and wrinkles. It's a famous camera shot for horror films. Adjust your office chair and/or use a box, book stack, or tripod to get the camera (maybe it is in your computer, phone, or laptop) at the proper level.

Find and look at the camera lens. If needed, place a sticker beside it to direct your eyes there. The natural tendency is to talk to participants while looking at them on screen. That can often make you appear to look down with no eye contact. All of us have seen people on news shows who appear on video calls and look off to the side the entire time they are addressing a national audience.

Have the camera at a distance that shows your face without being so close as to mimic objectionable "in your face" speaking in real life. Try to find a position that depicts a distance one would have in a typical close-up, one-on-one office conversation. (Note that if you are using an on-camera microphone, this could impact the placement. (You will read more on this in the Audio section below.)

Lighting

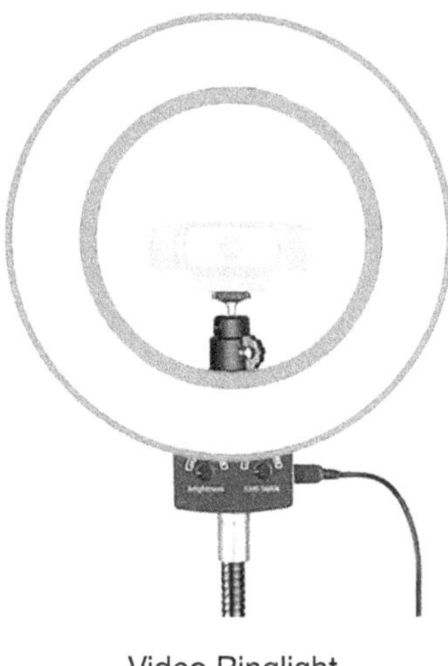

Video Ringlight

Lighting can make a huge difference in how you look in an online conference. Although we are not going for elegance here, just simply having the appearance of being alive, engaged and professional is a worthwhile goal. It can impact how much people pay attention to what you're saying.

The goal is to have as much even, full-face lighting as you can achieve. Lighting from below can cause all of the protrusions of your lower face to cast shadows on the upper face. Lighting from above accomplishes the opposite, with the shadows going downward. Both of those looks are better for a scary movie scene.

A window behind you can turn you into a mysterious

silhouette. Casting deep shadows on one side of your face deprives you of the full-face expressiveness that makes your comments more convincing. Computer devices generally cast a blue tint that can make you look more grey.

A soft incandescent light can fill in some of the shadows. A lot of online video professionals use a "Ring Light." It is a little circular light on a stand or tripod. With some, the "temperature" (or hue) of the light can be adjusted.

The best ones are LED and have a dimmer and light hue adjustment ability. These are designed to fill out the lighting for your face. (If your company has video professionals, they can advise on any other ways to do this, but go for simple, small and unobtrusive.)

Environment

This is not a movie set. Your goal should be to have the background as clean and uncluttered as possible. Standard wall adornments and room furnishings are okay if they're not distracting. You don't want people to ignore what you say while they are trying to find out what books you're reading from the shelf behind you.

Using a background capability built into an online program should be done with some evaluation of the message. (Most people don't do business standing by the San Francisco Bay Bridge.)

AUDIO

It's not uncommon to use the built-in mic on a laptop for online video. A rule of thumb to remember is that the closer you are to a microphone, the more it will screen out noises in the background. It is a balance. Being too close can overdrive the system and distort the sound.

Some choose to use small earphones and the microphone with those. Those mics tend to brush, or bounce, against clothing and create distracting noises. If you use one, find a small clip and attach it by the wire, a few inches below the mic, to a lapel or collar so it doesn't bounce around.

The microphone should pick up your voice without you dramatically leaning into it every time you talk. When you do lean in like that, your face suddenly gets larger than life in the video.

I once worked with a company that was planning an online encounter in which hundreds of millions of dollars could be at stake. They set this up in a small room with a fifteen-foot ceiling surrounded by windows at the top. This created a sound like a cavern. It was distracting and not at all professional-sounding. Instead of changing rooms, they covered the upper windows and experimented with audio devices to eventually overcome the impression of being lost souls in a cave.

Good, on-mic audio is important to credibility.

Voice/Gestures/Expressions for Video

Many people are tempted to speak loudly when they are in a virtual meeting. If that's necessary (because of poor audio), it's fine. If you are going to speak up, distinguish between increased volume and appearing to have excess passion.

Just increase the volume of your voice. Speak in a conversational voice and tone (not announcing or stiff). Remember, it's not a performance and you're not Alexander Graham Bell testing the first phone.

Gesture in a casual, normal manner. Just be sure your gestures are within the camera frame and not in front of your face. Relaxed gestures help add to the conversational nature of the meeting.

Too many people appear at these meetings with their arms

folded in a "V" under the table in front of them. This is awkward, brings your shoulders together and makes your body look out of proportion to your face. It also leaves your comments rather lifeless and not conversational at all.

The camera tends to understate your expressiveness. Don't over-emote, but make sure you have an energetic engagement. (Strangely, this can simply come from being energetically engaged.) Deadpan, washed-out expressions make for a long, boring meeting with little exchange of humanness, emotional investment, or respect.

SIXTEEN

Persuasion to Change

At the heart of conducting business and much of our personal lives is the ability to persuade others to make a change in their thinking and actions. All of the communication approaches we have described in this book contribute to this important element of success.

When we discuss finding a new paradigm for business communication, we must provide a formula for bringing about change.

For over fifty years, a valuable formula for change has been available, but unfortunately has not worked its way into current business culture and practice. This formula is certainly worth a reminder and revival in a search for a better communication paradigm.

The **Formula for Change** was created by David Gleicher in the early 1960s and later revised by Kathie Dannemiller in the 1980s. Dannemiller simplified the Gleicher formula by changing the letters in the equation to coincide better with the wording of the description.

We suggest updating and simplifying the designations even further, so the equation, as adapted, looks like this:

. . .

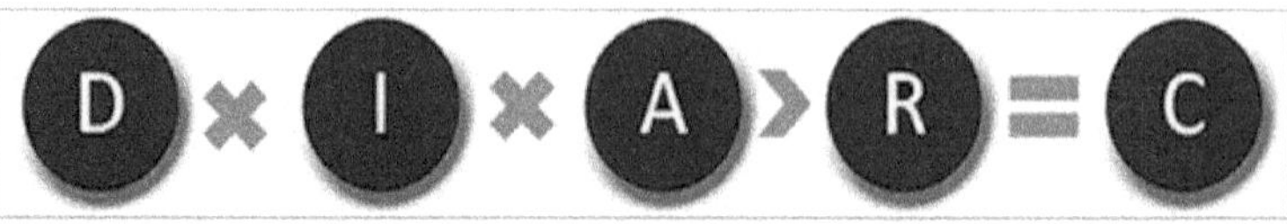

The factors as we now have them identified here are:

D = Dissatisfaction with the status quo
I = Imagery of a better end-state
A = Action required to move toward the goal
R = Resistance to the change
C = Change

An interpretation is that, in order to persuade for change, we would have to make sure that we meet an actual formula:

1. **D**issatisfaction with the status quo
2. Multiplied by a clear **I**mage of a better end state,
3. Multiplied by the ease of initiation for **A**ction required to achieve the change
4. Being greater than the **R**esistance to change
5. Will all tally to equal **C**hange.

(D x I x A > R = C)[1]

Obviously, before someone can create dissatisfaction with the status quo, it helps to define it. This means a first step for applying the formula is to do a very good job of specifically examining what the current circumstance or reality is.

In thirty-five years of business consulting, I've found it easy to identify that one of the biggest mistakes people make when they attempt to persuade others to change is not understanding or knowing enough about the status quo of their listener to be able to address it effectively.

The keys to effective implementation of the parts of this formula are contained in a previous chapter, where we discussed truth and what causes people to become convinced. The bottom line, of course, is that the factor that convinces people is the use of specifics cited from a source and in a way that an audience can trust, understand and embrace. Generalities don't sell.

Let's look at an example of a car sales agent trying to sell someone a new car.

Status Quo

It's important to know what the potential buyer is currently driving. How is it doing? If the salesperson knows some particular problems or quirks with that make and model of car, it could be helpful. If that seller doesn't know the details of the advantages of his/her own car over the buyer's current car, it could be a hard sell.

The salesperson would need to point out new features which one is sure the older car wouldn't have (desirable side warning indicators, ability to upload the digital phonebook to the onboard computer, a hundred thousand mile warranty).

The more specifically the prospective buyer can be made to understand how bad their auto status quo is (without insulting them), the more likely a sale. *The desire to want what one is missing is generated best by an understanding of the potential consequences of one's current state of deprivation.*

Clear Image of a Better End State

Notice that the formula is an equation, so the weighting of one section can be made up in another. We use "I" for imagery here because we want to create the ability of a listener to *see a clear image in their minds of this change, as if it has already taken place.*

Every good car salesperson knows that having the buyer test drive the car and actually picture themselves owning it, is a key element of the sale. The look, the feel, the warranty, the mileage, the safety and the prestige all can come into play.

This is, however, if they are presented as tangible specifics and not broad generalities. There is nothing much worse in sales than a car salesperson who doesn't know the specific features and advantages of the car they're selling. One must be able to create an image in the buyer's mind of them driving/owning that car.

Another example would be a good real estate agent who will ask the house seller to remove all of the family pictures and leave when the house is being shown. This maximizes the chance that the buyers can picture themselves living there. This section of the formula is most powerful when one can *very clearly create a picture of how things will be upon completion or fruition of the proposed change.*

I once showed this version of the Gleicher Formula for Change to a witness who was testifying about the costs for going to a four-year cycle of vegetation management tree cutting at a utility. This plan involved coming up with a proper schedule to keep tree growth out of power lines. His immediate response was, "Oh my God, I need to be showing them pictures as I describe this."

Where It Usually Falls Apart

From car selling to nuclear plant training to regulatory hearings, I've observed time and again that the greatest shortcoming of those who would exercise persuasion is the failure to know, understand and present in a crisp, clean way, strategically selected details of the status quo, the faults of that status quo and the clear, vivid picture of what the desired outcome will look like for the person being persuaded. If treated like math, doing it by the numbers can add up. Just like math, the numbers require specificity, and generalities don't stick or multiply well.

Action

The reason this piece in the formula is multiplied is that the convenience and ease with which someone can transition into the change has a weight in the decision-making. Change may not be digestible in huge chunks.

Some changes are big. Those changes may well take place in several steps. For example, driving the car, taking the car home for an overnight test drive, reading a comparison of cars, talking to the finance person, or getting pre-approved for a loan may all be actions that move toward the bigger auto purchase decision. It may very well be that the big leap into full devotion to the change comes after most resistance is gone.

For a politician, a desired action to trigger in a voter may be to get them to go to a website and look at where the candidate stands on policy. For a company witness, it could be to get the regulators to look more closely at numbers in an exhibit, or take time to more carefully understand a benchmarking study.

Most good real estate agents know that having a client get pre-approved for a house loan can be an important action taken early to influence the buyer to embrace the change of committing to a house deal.

Remember, this is a part of the formula we mentioned, so it has to be weighted to allow the parts to be greater than the resistance. In fact, onerous undertakings as first steps could kill the deal.

Resistance to Change

This is the ultimate driver of the formula. There can be no greater mistake in applying this formula of persuasion than misunderstanding, trivializing, or missing the details of the resistance.

As a young man, I had about a four-month period in which I tried my hand unsuccessfully at selling real estate part-time. For four weekends, I drove a family around (it's what was done in those days), looking at houses. I knew only to focus on and try to address their objections to each individual house. Finally, the couple had settled on a property and were starting to sign papers. Then the wife blurted out angrily, "Honey, I told you a year ago I have no intention of moving until Roy graduates from high school." (Roy was 10 at the time).

Any attempt at persuasion that is ignorant of, or that misunderstands, the details of the resistance has little chance of effectively applying the Formula for Change. A pharmaceutical witness testifying before a congressional committee where a committee member's child has had a serious problem with the drug being discussed had better know all about this fact going into the hearings.

If a utility line is planned to cross a utility commissioner's mother's property, one had better recognize a reason and potential for resistance in advance.

Resistance to change is the tipping point of the change equation, and the argument is stronger if one can openly and empathetically acknowledge the details of that resistance, then demonstrate strategically that the formula calculates a favorable comparison.

Unfortunately, in many forms, we are exposed every day to an epidemic of lazy selling by people who can't be bothered to understand the details of the sale.

At the same time, the explosion in the collection of data about individuals is being strategically used by some smart marketers such that they can know specifics about each of us and how they contribute to every part of the Formula for Change. The knowledge increases marketers' persuasive power over all of us as consumers (if the sellers know how to put it to work).

The Powerful Consequences of "No"

In most cases, when speakers want to be persuasive and prompt a change in thinking, they are trying for a "yes" from the hearer. It may be "yes" to a project, an idea or a proposed activity. The popular belief is that the most important goal is to convince the recipient of the myriad of benefits that a "yes" would bring.

One of the challenges is that saying "yes" can generally come with a price. The formula for change that is shown above in this chapter relies heavily on balancing dissatisfaction with the status quo against the costs of the benefits of the desired end-state

"No" can come with a great power of inertia. The comfort of no change can present a huge temptation. If it is perceived that only change comes with a cost, the likelihood of making the change is reduced. An important concept to introduce when trying to persuade someone to change is *the power of the consequence of "no."* This conveys the idea that rejection of an idea can also come with a cost.

The consequences of decision-making can weigh heavily on someone at the US Food and Drug Administration or the European Medicines Agency who has the responsibility to consider whether a drug is safe for use. There is an incredible amount of study put into the risk/benefit of the product. Most drugs come with risks. Most wouldn't reach the point of approval decisions if there weren't some benefit to some patients.

Individuals in both agencies have been burned at some point for supporting the approval of a product in which new risks were discovered after marketing. For such bureaucrats, such risks can present personal threats to career and possible humiliation and guilt. In most cases, "no" is the safest port for casting one's anchor.

The real challenge is to present a convincing argument that the refusal to grant the approval has very specific consequences. The more clearly one can present the negative consequences of the no vote, the more compelling is the argument for change. The closer to home those consequences can become, the more powerful the influence.

Another example of the powerful inertia of "no" is the circumstance of an elected State Utility Commissioner considering the case of a utility company wanting to build a new, innovative type of electric generating plant. Such a project would probably involve spending large amounts of ratepayers' money.

Certainly, innovation doesn't come easy to bureaucrats. The inertia of "no" is compelling. Here is an example where a clearly spelled out consequence of a no vote could help that elected official explain the vote to constituents. It could be that failure to provide a diversity of types of fuel used by the utility's plants could result in skyrocketing inflation in fuel costs.

It could be that the lack of the additional resource could put customers in the dark in the future. Perhaps refusal to create construction jobs could threaten votes in an important election precinct. A good, persuasive presenter would help that commissioner put together the perception and their own argument for the consequences of a no vote.

Sometimes, the clear enunciation of the consequences of

saying "no" must be made carefully, but clearly enough to help the hearer understand the entire picture of the path forward.

We can't be sure how much of this *Change Formul*a data is incorporated into AI outputs. We can address that in two ways. One is checking the response for *Change Formula* elements when asking AI to generate a narrative to persuade for a change in thinking to be made.

Another approach is to make sure that we put the status quo, the desirable end state, the resistance to change and the consequences of "no" in the initial AI prompt, to assure all of the information is there for an impactful response.

The ability for a successful presenter to persuade is the power to generate trust, create clear images of alternative outcomes, and make the path to initial implementation an easy one.

SEVENTEEN

Hitting a Moving Target

The matters of scaffolds and frames, attention spans and trust become quite a challenge for the communicator when we realize the target for how a recipient will perceive information is moving all the time. This chapter addresses some of the popular perceptions about the mental state of the receivers of communication with the goal of helping communicators design and implement clear and effective messaging.

What if Learning Styles Are a Myth?

One commonly held belief among educators and some psychologists since the early 1900s is that people have different learning styles. This theory can be characterized simply by listing several of the fundamental styles cited in the theory and suggesting people might be:

- **Visual** – learning through what they see
- **Auditory** – learning through what they hear
- **Tactile** – learning through hands-on experience

- **Kinesthetic** – requiring learning be reinforced by continuous movement

This theory has grown and evolved into what are now dozens of categories offered by almost a hundred different sources that believe they have identified a daunting number of additional learning styles.

In more recent years, researchers have begun to seriously question these theories. Harold Pashler at the University of California, San Diego, and others have published research demonstrating a general failure to scientifically validate the ability to identify and test learning styles.

Psychology researchers Daniel Willingham and Cedar Reiner argue that the data only support that differences in learning are attributable to differences in ability/intelligence, interests, or background knowledge.[1] Certainly, in directing any new information at an audience, at least these three factors must be taken into account.

There is a growing body of evidence that speakers and educators who pack their presentations with every kind of physical experience and sensation a receiver can have as a means of getting their point across to all the learning styles represented in an audience may be wasting a lot of time.

Rather than trying to consider learning styles, perhaps speakers are more successful when they consider (and style their presentations for) the audience differences in ability/intelligence, interests, or background knowledge. This demands some good understanding of the audience, and that is a good thing.

Speaking to the PAC

One theory of psychology that is a matter of less controversy, however, is the existence of ego states.

Psychiatrist Eric Berne is well known for his work with human ego states. Berne established that these ego states are real and observable results of brain programming that begins to run in certain ways at certain times as we interact with our world.

The ego states can affect feelings and behavior. In creating his Transactional Analysis approach to assessing human interaction, Berne identified these as the Parent, Adult and Child ego states, and those references became a part of popular culture.

The **Parent** represents those instances when people respond to circumstances as they observed their parents did or would. The **Adult** ego state is a more autonomous, practical and objective basis of evaluation in responding to circumstances. The **Child** ego state reaction is like the person would have responded to a similar circumstance when they were a small child. We are said to have inside us the potential for Parent, Adult, or Child to emerge at any time.[2]

Berne theorized, and years of observation in popular culture confirm, that humans constantly switch between these ego states as we react to the events around us.

One can be sure that ego states must be taken into account by anyone who wants their messages to stick with a recipient. It is most probably the prevailing ego state of the hearer in a given moment, more than a learning style, which impacts the effectiveness of teaching/learning interaction, as well as any more general communication of new information.

Are You Presenting Your Statistical Analysis to a Child?

Someone addressing an audience would be mistaken to assume the audience members are always in the same ego state as the speaker in every section of the speech. One also can't predict that individual audience members will always move in sync with others in the room from one ego state to the next.

The reality is that at any given moment during the presentation, individual audience members may be in any of the ego states at any time. The most critical explanation of the most complicated part of a presentation could fall on the ears of audience members who are lost in a sexual fantasy, or having childlike thoughts.

A speaker should never expect that an audience will give full attention, locked in adult ego state, to a twenty-minute talk on a strictly numerical account of last year's sales figures that is written in lackluster bulleted text slides. That would require the whole audience to stay in the adult ego state for the entire twenty minutes. While presenters of important information can frequently expect exactly that, frankly, it's impossible.

One of the most formal, stodgy and demanding presentations of data one can find often takes place at a federal drug approval hearing. I recall arguments among medical scientists involved in those hearings because pharmaceutical sponsor teams wanted to switch from black and white overhead projectors to colored slide presentations. Scientific conservatives considered the "flashy" slides to be "unscientific" and unprofessional.

Some of their objections were overcome a few years later when presentations switched from slide to digital, but suspicions of being "too flashy" remained if there happened to be color, or movement, or anything other than bullet slides, graphs, or tables. The irony was that these scientists were totally ignoring the fact that there is also a science of communication.

Often, people see themselves as authorities on how such presentations should be made when they have almost no knowledge or appreciation for neurolinguistics, communication psychology nor other communication scientific research.

There exists in some professions what one might call a "sustained adult state theory"- an assumption that a *disciplined* mind will remain in adult mode even during hours upon hours of a discussion. By simply observing one of the drug approval meetings described here, one can disprove the constant adult state theory.

At those hearings, one sees the frequent emergence of child and parent ego states in movements, expressions and the comments of the participants. I have found this to be true in thousands of various formal business discussions. Even with the most disciplined minds, the thought of a constant adult state is a myth. Berne was right. People constantly switch from one ego state to another.

Acknowledgment of the need to accommodate changing ego states would help participants make more sense of the data they see and probably make for better scientific decisions. The way to deal with changing ego states in an audience is to expect, or even cause them, by making changes in the style of the presentation that accommodate ego state shifts.

When science decides to put into practice in its own communication what research reveals about the science of the mind and attention span and communication, the world will be a better place.

When one shoots a gun at a moving target without accounting for the movement, the shot will probably miss. To be successful, the shooter would have to be in motion to track the movement of the target. It could certainly be an option to just keep shooting in the same place in hopes the target would run in front of the gun occasionally, but that would be inefficient, frequently unsuccessful and a waste of time and ammunition.

That is certainly similar to what happens when a speaker expects an audience to lock in on a single ego state during an entire presentation. It simply wastes informational ammunition.

Miraculously, even in stark, formal scientific meetings, occasionally a speaker might do what some would consider "breaking the tension" by making a light-hearted comment or urging some participation by the audience.

These more successful speakers are generally more appreciated and effective because they facilitate an inevitable ego state change in each of their audience members. This accommodation allows for a return to focus and more time in the desired ego state for the desired transfer of data to the audience.

The impacts of rapid ego state shifts are seen in the most popular media presentations. The most successful movies jerk the audience in and out of various ego states in rapid sequence. Recent research indicates that human attention span is getting shorter. Some attribute this to exposure to the internet and other forms of media.

Very rapid instigation of switching from parent to child ego states in popular news and entertainment features may be creating a more volatile and frequent auto-shifting of the ego states in the population.

This places even more constraints on the presenter who is presuming an audience member will remain in the same state for an extended period.

What Does This All Mean for a Communicator?

The communicator has to find ways to accommodate the ego state shift in listeners. If one were to conduct an exhaustive study and determine to learn transactional analysis well enough to calculate every interaction, it could be possible to engage in communication in a way that tracks and responds to all of this shifting around. But, such an approach would probably seriously damage the communicator's ability to be spontaneous, human, transparent and authentic.

A better approach is to address the ego state changes by stimulating them. Speaking in the Parent ego state involves words of critique, admonition, concern, comfort and other commentary we might expect from a parent.

The Adult ego state speaks in questions, reasoned statements, objective opinions, beliefs, data lists and straightforward information exchanges.

The Child ego provides a break in the mundane, a recess, a laugh, other spontaneous emotions, delight, wishes, stories, references to colors, rebellion and other vivid expressions such as one might see in children.

A communicator who recognizes the moving target of ego states would know not to expect an audience to stay in parent or adult, or even child ego states for a long period of time. The authenticity of the speaker allows their own ego states to transition appropriately, and the audience to follow. These speakers appear as open, human, approachable and embraced by an audience.

This variation and accommodation of changes in ego states is what makes some speakers so much more interesting than others. Some of the best jokes, some of the most powerful stories, some of the finest presentations are those that carry us along in one ego state, then quickly *snap us into another*. Audiences tend to love the surprise and to enthusiastically take this journey with the presenter.

People's minds are always in motion. Their attention is not static, and the gifted speaker knows how to entice, challenge and intrigue the listener by moving with them or ahead of them.

EIGHTEEN

Choosing Language for a Growth Mindset

In the current business world, we have seen a dizzying fluctuation in attitudes. When this book was first written in 2016, we were seeing a change from command and control to more free and innovative employee engagement. Then, between the COVID years, attacks on Diversity, Equity and Inclusion (DEI) and a new, more hostile, political rhetoric, we have found ourselves in a situation where corporate culture is more frequently more dependent on the political and social mindset of the leadership of the organization. Brashness, meanness and even insults are newly popularized as somehow empowering.

These mindset shifts have been reflected in language. As humans, our language defines us. Too often we make use of language that is limiting, uninspired and even failure-promoting. Regardless of politics or social motivation, there is a scientific linguistic reality of how language engages and moves people.

The next generation of powerful communicators will know how to speak a language for growth, the language of becoming. It is also a language of individual respect.

We acknowledge that discretion must be applied when determining when to use fixed, versus growth language. That is discussed later in this chapter. What we do want to assert here is that a constantly fixed mindset approach is not efficiently productive in today's environment.

In 2006, Stanford University Psychologist Dr. Carol Dweck wrote a profound book detailing what she referred to as "fixed" versus "growth" mindsets. Broad application of Dweck's ideas have come under some fire, but we will discuss in this chapter a selective and strategic use of her concepts.

Fixed

The fixed mindset is based on the belief that people are either intelligent or they are not, talented or they are not, gifted with abilities or not. Believing in a fixed mindset, individuals always find themselves struggling to win, to succeed, or to prove something.

In adversity, or failure, or faced with the success of others, employees or students may give up early, avoid challenges, bristle at negative feedback and grow frustrated in competition. In this setting, people can dig in their heels and refuse to develop allegiances. All of this is because success or failure seems to define them as a person. In the fixed mindset, failure is often seen as an identity. Success is seen as a more temporary identity.

Growing

The growth mindset provides a much different, more positive perspective. Rather than being identified by outcomes, the individual believes any results are stepping stones to the next level of growth. These individuals anticipate and embrace challenge, persevere, give extra effort, gain insight from mistakes, value criticism and in difficulty celebrate, study, and learn from the success of others.[1]

There are powerful implications here for effective communication. Unfortunately, most education systems and businesses operate in a way that counts on and promotes a fixed mindset. Innate abilities are expected and celebrated.

One may frequently hear how gifted, talented, or particularly effective someone is on a job. Others may be defined as not suited, or not smart or talented enough, having limited abilities, or simply being ineffective. Success and failure in a fixed mindset organization tend to have clear definitions and consequences.

The very idea of personnel being disposable is one of the consequences of a fixed mindset in business. The idea that talent and ability are innate and people can just be exchanged for new ones when their abilities have been exhausted or they find their limits, is highly destructive.

This is especially true in a competitive environment thriving on creativity, innovation and outside-the-box thinking.

Fixed mindset businesses frequently drive employees to the point of underestimating their capabilities and hitting the wall of their innate talent.

All of this is exacerbated by detached, posturing language that mercilessly pushes the employee to compete to a point of ultimate failure. It is also coupled with piling work into the job definition to an ultimate point of assured failure. Too many people in business are in a situation where they are loaded to the point of failure, then sometimes discarded.

The Agricultural and Industrial Ages had an important stake in people being fixed at what they were trained and positioned in life to be. English surnames, for example, reflect the static, often generational aspect of fixed identity. Potter, Miller, Smith, Baker, Brewer, Carpenter, Mason, Miner, Tinker,

Weaver and many other family names were attached to a specific profession and sometimes destined generations to be fixed in that field of work.

When the Industrial Revolution came along, there was no reason for a manufacturing plant to want an assembly line worker to envision an identity beyond that occupation. Certainly, there were apprentices who were becoming adept in a specific field of work, but the goal was always a specific and static state of being that was based on talent and indoctrination to perform one job.

An hierarchical command and control system identified the limits and rewarded only conformity. Built around this approach, a language of fixed "being" developed. One could be a "skilled" worker (as opposed to an "unskilled" worker). Unfortunately, the language often defined an identity for some, rather than a level of achievement.

The hierarchical business model that encouraged fixed identities rather than growth identities is disappearing fast. The incredible speed at which business is moving and the increasing necessity for innovation are challenging the hierarchical structure. Increasingly, "fixed" roles can be conducted by some version of robotics and artificial intelligence.

Our current reality is a new environment that demands an awareness that to quickly think, initiate and innovate must be distributed among human team members who are working with the efficiency of AI interaction.

In a strict command and control organization, innovative ideas are seldom accepted from the middle and lower-level employees. In such a management structure, even mediocre ideas from the bosses can be met with praise, promotion and expenditure (in the dance of bowing to power). This is because those in charge are assumed to have reached their fixed positions because of some specific, static, measured talent. This is all being challenged by technology.

So many businesses are now left with one foot on the shore of stodgy hierarchy and one foot on the ship that is sailing daily for the new world of innovative competition.

The big question for them is: "How do I safely make a transition?" Imagine going into the board of a very conservative multi-billion dollar utility company and claiming that tomorrow you are going to distribute much of what has been the command and control leadership and decision-making "through the ranks." Imagine proclaiming that you are shifting to a language of "Growth Mindset" and want everybody on board. Bless your heart if you think that will work.

One can argue the value proposition for distributed leadership convincingly, but still not account for the risk to a large corporation that can be part of making that kind of transition. Certainly, a distributed leadership approach is easier for startups, and maybe that's why so many are so successful.[2]

Unmistakably, the shift to more integrated robotic technology is going to demand a review and revision of how we approach and engage the human element of our corporate cultures. The role and definition of that element is destined to change now at dizzying speed. Can we keep up?

Change The Language, Change the Culture

We should note here that a generational and societal shift has brought a strange integration of communication expectations to the workplace. Leadership must establish its business culture through communication example, and in an AI world, the human touch is increasingly more unique and important.

One way to start to make a transition to distributed leadership is to recognize the difference between the language that defines the fixed and the growth mindset. This may mean revisiting our framing, symbolism and language choices in schools and in business.

In a 2014 Ted Talk, Dr. Carol Dweck praised a school for changing the language of grading. Rather than giving children an “F” for failing, the school was giving a “Not Yet.”[3] The messages in the difference in language are enormous. Notice this is not like saying: “We’re going to pass you to the next level and reward you anyway,” as some schools are doing. It is not like giving a trophy for “participation.” This is simply saying: “You don’t know this material yet, keep working on it.” The result was a new motivation for students to improve.

Fixed mindset organizations define fixed mindset people with day-to-day language. No matter how seemingly innately “talented” he or she may be, a fixed mindset person is, in many cases, pushed to the point of failure and the ultimate definition of their limitations. Growth becomes impossible because language reinforces the fixed boundaries.

In many fixed mindset organizations with fixed mindset people, growth mindset language may be seen as patronizing or over the top. You, the readers, are encouraged to review your own set of business and personal words to examine the impacts they have. You may also want to evaluate your own self-talk to determine whether you are stuck in a fixed mindset trap. I

When one may not want to lean heavily on *Growth Mindset:*

- In high-stakes or urgent situations, clarity and directness matter more than framing.
- Compliance, legal, or safety communication where growth framing can sound vague or permissive when precision is required. (For example, we can look at an industry like the nuclear industry, where instructions are so critical that they must be repeated by the recipient to ensure they were heard

correctly. One could not just say, "Might I suggest we will soon want to turn valve B236H7." At the same time, the need for specificity and quick response may make that industry one of those that is ripe for AI introduction.

- In cases when bluntness serves specific purpose to convey the seriousness of a matter. [This should be measured and used deliberately to punctuate a need or circumstance.])

Some people explicitly prefer direct, neutral, or even stark language. In those cases, excessive growth framing can feel patronizing or evasive. This can also vary by profession.

We acknowledge that sometimes *Growth Mindset* language can backfire:

- If it minimizes real frustration ("This was just a challenging assignment.")
- If it avoids accountability
- If it sounds like optimism without action

One can work to avoid these circumstances by pairing growth language with specific communication of next steps, constraints, or decisions.

The bottom line here, of course, is that we are now in a society that is engaged in a process to reinvent our language to adapt to a heavily overhauled version of business relationships and expectations brought on by societal changes and technology.

A popular reaction by some has been to just fight paradigm shifts by doubling down on Fixed Mindset management. There is a new wave of authoritarian leadership destined to backfire with a new workforce generation.

A move from a fixed mindset to a growth mindset is quite a

challenging cultural change to accomplish in a company. A first step for leadership in such a company can be awareness of the language of limitation, failure, frustration and detachment that can permeate a fixed mindset team. Approaching leadership with this awareness and beginning to change the language can start to redefine realities and begin to move attitudes.

In some instances, just awareness and avoidance of language that is destructive of growth mindset may trigger a move to a more desirable environment.

Growth Mindset phrases are:

- Seeking
- Forward-looking
- Encouraging
- Respectful
- Appropriately challenging
- Affirming
- Supportive
- Truthful
- Inquisitive
- Searching

Here are a few examples of how people communicate these fixed or growth states in language every day:

Words of Fixed Mindset (Examples)

- Stuck
- Limited
- Lost
- Failed
- Given up

- Stymied
- Can't
- Won't
- Shouldn't
- Unqualified
- Incapable
- Clueless
- Loser
- It is what it is
- Limited
- Overwhelmed

Words of Growth Mindset (Examples)

- Evolving
- Dynamic
- Participatory
- Become
- Grow
- Develop
- Learn
- Progress
- Rising
- Motivating
- Seeking
- Discovering
- Inspired
- Mentor
- Questioning

Unfortunately, the educational system in the United States appears to have embraced a fixed mindset curriculum that is producing too many fixed mindset graduates. Teaching to a test, suppressing inquiry and singling out "gifted" students to be separated from others results in turning out a product that encourages too much of a fixed mindset approach to life and business.

Today, cultural/social movements are challenging the teaching of critical thinking for students in advanced education institutions. That is a dangerous position in a world where humans must have a role as the ultimate critical thinkers in terms of morality and human impacts.

Certainly, one should define fixed levels and measurements of success in education and in business. Those milestones should be seen more as plateaus, rather than ultimate goals.

As an example, the difference between Paul McCartney of *The Beatles* and other "few-hit-wonders" in the music business is that McCartney never stopped growing, developing his music styles and evolving his identity as a musician.

Joseph Evans is an internationally renowned opera tenor. He has taught some of the brightest, most successful young opera singers in the business and has authored the definitive handbook on teaching opera. Evans describes what it means to have a plateau:

There was a point in my singing career when I knew I had met all the measures of success that might have been set for me. I was performing in all the best opera houses in the world and getting all the best parts. I wasn't satisfied with that. I came to the realization that in order to remain inspired, I had to always be learning. I learned new parts, I took on new roles and challenged my capabilities. Only then did I find the most fulfilling career excitement.[4]

That quest for learning and growth didn't stop there. Evans has gone on to become one of the leading academic authorities in the world on the mechanisms of vocal capacity and development.

Business leaders who are satisfied with the goals and the language of fixed mindset are hugely shortchanging the potential of their employees and their business endeavors. They may very well also be ill-equipped to handle the new juxtaposition between robotic/AI elements and the creative human side of staffing. New definitions of the expanded boundaries for success may well be on the horizon. A totally fixed mindset organization will miss them.

At the same time, a growth mindset involves invested, creative thinking, and insistence on that kind of thinking could come as quite a shock to some work cultures.

Business is changing rapidly in a direction that will increasingly demand growth mindset philosophies and individuals. In a highly technological, AI world, fixed Mindset language is on a collision course with the need to generate emotional investment by the humans involved in work. A good leader has to have great discernment of what language to choose for each situation. Leadership's use of AI may not always be able to tune into the subtleties.

As humans, our words define our reality. One can bet that the reality of a dynamic, growing, learning organization will now more than ever be set in place by an evolution in its language.

~

NINETEEN

Pandemic and Politics

For several years now, business people have been dealing with what I call, COVID PTSD (Post Traumatic Stress Syndrome).

For two years, we did not know if or when we might catch a disease that could kill us. Some saw relatives, friends and acquaintances die from COVID-19. Some have become ill and survived. There were images of semi-trailer trucks serving as morgues at hospitals.

The public was bombarded with a constant drone of debates, warnings and coverage of international struggle with an invisible threat that had killed millions. Some had incomes cut and careers disrupted. Through it all, many people were also cut off from traditional social norms, public interactions and usual patterns of life routines.

When the Twin Towers in New York were brought down by aircraft, there followed a general consensus that all of the United States was experiencing a common, shared trauma. The stress and disruptions that followed changed US society forever.

Little has been said about the new perceptions of threat and the common experience of impending trauma and serious disruption that two years of pandemic and upheaval brought to us worldwide. Instead, we have been anxious to return to normal patterns and pretend we have no lasting psychological impacts. We are interacting with each other with little regard for the fact that pronounced and prolonged trauma can bring depression, isolation, anger, magic-thinking, detachment from reality, intolerance, loss of empathy, general aggression, malaise, indifference and much more.

Whatever one's political leanings, we must admit that the pandemic experience was followed by even more insecurity with economic uncertainty, then deep political upheaval and division. This, not to mention the controversy surrounding vaccines and the continued threat of various virus variations.

There can be a commonality of responses experienced by a society that together undergoes prolonged PTSD. Research suggests this may account for migration toward more self-protective thinking. When there is a common societal trauma, collective traumatization may lead to increases in:

1

Conservatism	Erosion of empathy
Isolationism	Hostility for alternative views
Heightened feeling of distrust *(1)*	Feelings of injustice
Depression	

COVID Impacts on Business

Researchers are well aware that sustained, collective threat and trauma can leave societies vulnerable to social, political and financial upheaval. Many businesses are experiencing threat fatigue, and despite the disruptive nature of our common COVID-19 and political upheaval experiences, we are all longing for normalcy.

Many of us are willing to apply whatever strange self-hypnosis may go into pushing to restore everything to the way it was. This, even if it ignores the threat and perpetuates the pandemic and/or social upheaval.

Some reluctantly returned to working in an office. Employees were jammed back into the work environment with little recognition that we may all be changed. If we are to be productive in our communication, we must have a new awareness that the people we know may have lives impacted by trauma we don't know or understand. This is compounded by a severely politically divided populace in a rapidly changing geopolitical environment.

We may experience less devotion to cognitive engagement, less tolerance for differences of opinion, or faster refusal to invest emotions.

Virtual sessions include participants with differing levels of audio clarity, varying ability in navigating the environment and usually unrealistic and sometimes oppressive time targets and pressures.

Recently, a woman in an important position with a high-tech firm expressed frustration that she was forced to be online for an hour and a half meeting where a consultant was announcing a company requirement that everyone now had to learn about and be tolerant of neurodiversity in their workplace. "I'm booked with meetings all day long," she said, "I'm still struggling with long-term COVID brain fog myself, can't always understand what my colleagues are trying to say, and now I am asked to recognize and somehow adjust my interactions to neurodiversity with no clarity as to how I am supposed to do that? Was I required to be made to understand and recognize this all in an hour and a half meeting, where everyone was talking? I can't even..."

Hers is a classic frustration, lowered empathy, and even anger with the seemingly out-of-control process of a world trying to act like everything is normal. Amid all of this psychosocial disruption, employees are forced to be productive, to communicate creatively and to continue contributions to our own and our employer's financial well-being.

The times call for a new look at communication in the workplace. We must contend with the possibilities of reduced levels of personal investment, amplified distractions, increased levels of intolerance and heightened vigilance for a potential for injustice. We are all a little fragile and a little prickly. The experience of two years of confrontation with our own mortality has changed many people's priorities. That population then entered a time of deep political and social division. Many people in the US must have PTSD.

To communicate in a communal PTSD environment, we should remember several things:

Don't

- Don't use this vulnerable time to try to climb over others in the organization. The typical office game of diminishing the influence of others to enhance one's own rise to the top is counterproductive, blatant and ill-conceived in an age of PTSD. Others will spot you fast, resent you wasting their time and "get" you at the earliest opportunity.
- Don't be fooled if you get casual, uninvested agreement from people who just don't give a damn what you do. They may have no intention of supporting your concepts in actual work or practice.
- Don't talk fast and in so much jargon and verbiage that people are compelled to just pretend they are hearing. We are all slower now.
- Don't expect immediate buy-in. Everyone is more

suspicious; everyone is more resistant to change, and everyone is more defensive with PTSD.

Do

- Hear others. There is a great need to be heard, and an underlying hope that something an individual says will make a difference to someone somewhere. The recipient of this experience of having been heard can actually be enriched by the exchange with immeasurable rewards. The concentration and effort toward understanding all of the elements of another's discourse is the great difference between listening and hearing. A consideration of the power of being heard also speaks of the growing dangers of the use of detached, digital texting that encourages more listening than hearing. This is particularly true in a time of PTSD. (2)
- Be very clear with your statements. Tell us up front where you are taking us. Put the bottom line up front. Tell us what you are trying to prove or the point you are trying to make, then talk slowly and clearly enough to give your PTSD-ridden friends time to take it in as you go through the details.
- Find some opportunity at some time for (outside of office issue discussion) personal feedback, and virtual visiting with colleagues. The asides and hallway discourse in live office environments bring personalization to relationships and a chance to sort out context for business comments. Missing that context in a virtual environment is amplified and deadly in PTSD-fired virtual business

interchanges that are held under enormous time pressures.

- Cut others some slack, don't jump on little mistakes or misstated meanings. We are all distracted in hundreds of ways. Audio may be "breaking up." The cat may have jumped on the piano, and one may have missed some of the points of a discussion. In a very real way, with the distraction of PTSD, we are all playing catch-up all the time. Ask people what they meant, or say you are making sure you heard it correctly.
- Create a reasonable agenda for virtual meetings and make sure there is a backup time for what was not covered. It's easy to overestimate what can be covered in a hard hour. An aggressive agenda can leave out valuable input, create tune-out and arrive at conclusions that are poorly vetted. Make input, participation and discussion time count.
- Put your own and others' frustration and anger into the proper perspective. We all have a right to be angry and frustrated all the time right now. Let's ease up on each other.
- Do a quick summary at the top of the meeting of what you expect to cover, and a quick list at the end of what was decided and path forward objectives. Make intentions clear for foggy-headed victims of communal PTSD or long-term COVID.

We will all recover from the traumas of our time. It's a time to be aware of our common struggles and help each other return to a normal work and living environment. It's a time to be nice.

TWENTY

A Most Dangerous World (and the power of humanity)

Communication in our world is not in a particularly good state. What is needed is a new appreciation of our mutual humanity. In social and business associations, humankind has the capacity (through the powerful communication advantages technology has brought to us) to embrace a break with some old language and cultural barriers.

A new communication paradigm would be bound together by our integrity.

Unfortunately, we are in a transition period where we are experiencing what we might call "AI communication creep." Artificial Intelligence is, not so gradually, creeping into our business communication in a way that is becoming more and more pervasive and more and more difficult to recognize. It is doing so with little formal guidance and great variability in individuals' understanding.

Artificial Intelligence is coming on fast!

At the time of this tenth anniversary update of this book, Artificial Intelligence is growing dramatically in business. By 2025, between 78% and 88% of companies globally reported using AI in at least one business function, up from 55% in 2023.[1,2]

Business outcomes can be documented:

• 71% of organizations using AI in marketing and sales report revenue gains

• 63% see increases in supply chain management[3]

• Over 19% of companies saw revenue increases exceeding 10% from AI in supply chain and inventory management[4]

AI is also more frequently used for strategy, corporate finance (21%) and content creation (63%)[5]

By late 2025, approximately one in six people worldwide were using generative AI tools[6] AI is increasingly becoming technically embedded in the tools of our lives. For example, the FDA approved 223 AI-enabled medical devices in 2023, up from just six in 2015. The trend at the FDA continued in 2025 despite dramatic changes in the agency.[7,8] Autonomous vehicles are also becoming more common.[9]

According to *Pew Research Center* (2025), 78% of Americans are aware of AI, with 45% expressing concern about its impact on jobs and society.[10] A Harvard study found a 13% decline in employment for workers aged 22–25 in AI-exposed fields since 2022. By 2030, AI is expected to create 170 million new jobs and replace 92 million. Somehow, it is claimed that this resulted in a net gain of 78 million jobs globally.[11]

We must acknowledge that a great deal of business communication is now generated by AI. We must admonish readers to inject humanity and reality into the output of such generated communication.

First, edit to make sure the AI document represents your style and meaning. Next, be aware that AI may not always understand the subtle circumstances of a communication.

Make sure your prompts to the AI source are clear as to the intent and audience for the message. Check the output for meaningful message framing that is on-target with your intent. Look for accuracy in elements of proof of claims.

While the convenience of simply cranking out an AI message under time pressure is unquestionable, the long-range impacts for business of having what amounts to someone else (the Large Language Model) represent you can compromise relationships. This can cause your identity to be awash in routine or repeated jargon or narratives that aren't representative at all of your tone and humanity.

In a world where machines will be able to interpret all our intentions, it may be the intentions of those who control the machines that become suspect. The technical ability to process endless video of humans and read intent and emotion through analysis of speakers, being able to catalogue with great detail the opinions and actions of millions of individuals, brings a new expediency for each of us in society to demonstrate authenticity of thought and purpose.

The goal for an improved communication paradigm must include people having the care and personal investment to be responsive to each other. This century's successful communicators will address others with respect and inquire for mutually-understood symbols and examples to assure clarity in interactions. human experience may b getting lost in the shuffle.

As an example we can again point to the electric utility industry. New programs provide a highly innovative way to file documents such as regulatory rate cases. AI can quickly scan historical filings and rulings, testimony and claims and generate a highly-informed output for a new filing with a regulatory commission.

This was previously done by company personnel, many of whom learned a lot more about the business in the course of their research. One could ask if a lot of the process of accumulation of corporate knowledge is being sacrificed in having access to almost immediate data generation in the new approach. (Does that create a differently-purposed employee.) At the same time, one could ask, "Does it matter now?"

To love someone is to aspire for the loved one to find fulfillment, to be all they can become. Rather than a destructive mindset of fixed, competitive, limiting expectations, those in a healthy society embrace a growth mindset of mutual encouragement, enthusiastic innovation and a celebration of endeavor. That kind of society uses language that is expanding rather than limiting, affirming, respectful, invested and intended to inform for progress.

In that kind of environment, there is an enormous relief of the pressure of having to constantly position oneself to be important to one's peers. Imagine an office setting where all of the intrigue and competitive interaction of fixed mindset dialogue were removed. Imagine a world in which individuals find themselves enthusiastically invested in each other's growth and success.

Imagine a company in which the corporate "self" is mindful of what the needs are for nutrition and care for all of its body parts and encourages transparency and candid dialogue.

Defining Our Humanity

We as humans don't have much time to incorporate new, higher communication standards into our daily reality. Supercomputing and artificial intelligence will soon have the ability to read and report on even the slightest nuances in our movements, expressions and language.

These capabilities for interpreting our myriad methods of

interaction will either hold enormous potential for clarity, peace and understanding of true purpose, or will expose us as the detached, cynical, narcissists we may, without some form of intervention, soon become.

The technology that has provided multiple channels of interaction, facilitating clandestine social fracturing, can also unite us in a new recognition of dignity, openness and mutual respect.

In many ways, we as humans are what we don't say. The willingness to be deliberate, thoughtful, caring, authentic, transparent and devoted to truth in the mental process that precedes the words that come out of our mouths or go to the keyboard is what shapes the way our interactions identify us.

Often, it's the words and ideas that are excluded in that process that define our integrity and identity in business. Willingness to listen to others in a way that gains insight into the motivation and basis of their understanding before we interrupt them or attempt to convince them also defines us as individuals.

One of my hobbies is watercolor painting. A challenging lesson in learning to paint is the importance and power of unfilled spaces on the paper. Watercolor artists have to protect those spaces, leaving them unblemished until the end of the painting, so they bring the work to life as the highlights and sources of brilliance for the work.

Machines may learn to speak as humans speak, to express emotions as we express emotions, to match our phrasing and our tone and to sound quite like us. What they may never capture is the humanity and intellect behind the words.

Humanity will for many years to come have an exclusivity on the ability for an identity beyond the spoken word. We alone will retain the ability to provide that powerful, unblemished space on the artist's canvas. That brilliant, untouched highlight of the watercolor painting is like the magic of the word unspoken and the value of the healing power of hearing. That is our place in the future.

Limit of Liability/Disclaimer of Warranty:

The author and publisher have used best efforts to prepare this book, but we make no representations or warranties with respect to the accuracy or completeness of its contents.

The book contains approaches and strategies that may not be suitable for every unique business situation.

No specific warranty is made for the applicability to your business, nor the business success of adopting of any suggestion herein. Readers should make their own assessment of each situation in light of the details at that moment. The contents herein are intended to be food for thought.

Note that internet websites offered as citations may have changed between the time this book was written and when it is read.

Notes

1. A Disturbing Status Quo

1. 1 Weber Shandwick. (2016) Nearly All Likely Voters Say Candidates' Civility Will Affect Their Vote; New Poll Finds 93% Say Behavior Will Matter. [Press Release]. Retrieved from http://webershandwick.com/news/article/nearly-all-likely-voters-say-candidates-civility-will-affect-their-vote
2. 2 George, Dan, Chief. Used with the permission of his brother Leonard George, who I contacted in 2014.

2. Successfully Mean?

1. 3 Shu, Amy Jen. Get Over Your Fear of Conflict. HBR Blog Network. June 6, 2014. Retrieved from http://blogs.hbr.org/2014/06/get-over-your-fear-of-conflict/
2. 4 Whitbourne, Susan Krauss, Ph.D., Shedding Light on Psychology's Dark Triad A dirty dozen tests to detect narcissism, Machiavellianism and psychopathy. Psychology Today. January 26, 2013. Retrieved from https://www.psychologytoday.com/blog/fullfillment-any-age/201301/shedding-light-psychology-s-dark-triad
3. Babiak, Paul Ph.D. and Hare, Robert, Ph.D., Snakes in Suits: When Psychopaths Go to Work. New York: Harper Business reprint. New York, New York. 2007. Preface xii
4. Daley, J. F., Goldstein, J., & Markowitz, M. (2011). Horrible Bosses [Film]. United States: New Line Cinema.
5. Namie, Gary. Christopher, Daniel. &Phillips, David. 2014 WBI U.S. Workplace Bullying Survey. Workplace Bullying Institute. (2014) p.3.
6. BullyingStatistics.org. Do You Have Workplace Bullies at Your Job. Retrieved from http://www.bullyingstatistics.org/content/workplace-bullying.html
7. Department of Labor, Bureau of Labor Statistics. Consensus of Fatal Occupational Injuries. September 17, 2015. Retrieved from http://www.bls.gov/iif/oshwc/cfoi/cftb0298.pdf
8. Department of Labor, Bureau of Labor Statistics. *Consensus of Fatal Occupational Injuries*. April 22, 2015. Retrieved from http://www.bls.gov/iif/oshwc/cfoi/cftb0278.pdf
9. Davenport, N., Schwartz, R. D., & Elliott, G. P. (1999). *Mobbing: Emotional abuse in the American Workplace*. Ames, IA: Civil Society Pub.

10. The University of British Columbia Sauder School of Business (MAY 29, 2014). Ostracism More Damaging Than Bullying In the Workplace. [Press Release]. Retrieved from http://news.ubc.ca/2014/05/29/better-to-be-bullied-than-ignored-in-the-workplace-study/

3. Are We Keepers?

1. Rand, Ayn. (1992)[1957]. Atlas Shrugged (35th anniversary ed.). New York: Dutton. "About The Author" p. 1170.
2. Blackwell, D. L., Lucas, J. W., & Clarke, T. C. (2014). Summary health statistics for U.S. adults: National Health Interview Survey, 2012: Data from the National Health Interview Survey. Hyattsville, MD: U.S. Dept. of Health and Human Services, Centers for Disease Control and Prevention, National Center for Health Statistics.
3. Wiktionary. (January 24, 2016). Wikipedia. Retrieved from https://en.wiktionary.org/wiki/altruism

4. Complicated Track to Communication Trouble

1. United States Patent and Trade Mark Office. U.S. Patent Activity Calendar Years 1790 to the Present - Table of Annual U.S. Patent Activity Since 1790. Retrieved from http://www.uspto.gov/web/offices/ac/ido/oeip/taf/h_counts.htm
2. Mauboussin, Michael J. What Shareholder Value is Really About. HBR Blog Network. October 3, 2011. Retrieved from http://blogs.hbr.org/2011/10/ceos-must-understand-what-crea/
3. United States Securities and Exchange Commission (July 22, 2010). SEC Charges Dell and Senior Executives With Disclosure and Accounting Fraud.[Press Release]. Retrieved from http://www.sec.gov/press/2010-131.htm
4. *Oak Ridge Institute for Science and Education.* "Nuclear Engineering Enrollment and Degrees Survey - 2021-2023 (updated February, 2024)." Number 84.1. found at: https://orise.orau.gov/stem/workforce-studies/reports/ne-brief-84-2022-data.pdf
5. By Yusuf Khan, "Shortage of Young Engineers Threatens Nuclear Renaissance." *WSJ PRO.* 11 September 2024.
6. U.S. Energy Information Administration. "U.S. Nuclear Reactor Shutdown List." Found at: http://www.nrc.gov/reading-rm/doc-collections/fact-sheets/decommissioning.html
7. State of New York Department of Financial Services (June 30, 2014). Cuomo Administration Announces BNP Paribas To Pay 8.9 Billion, Including 2.24 Billion To NYDFS, Terminate Senior Executives, Restrict US Dollar Clearing Operations For Breaking Law.[Press Release]. Retrieved from http://www.dfs.ny.gov/about/press2014/pr1406301.htm

8. Ibid.
9. BNP Paribas (July 31,2014). BNP Paribas Strengthens Its Control Over Mechanisms. [Press Release]. Retrieved 8-10-2014 from http://www.bnpparibas.com/en/news/press-release/bnp-paribas-strengthens-its-control-mechanisms
10. Reich, Robert. Rebirth of stakeholder capitalism. August 9, 2014. Robert Reich Blog. Retrieved from http://robertreich.org/post/94260751620
11. Solis, Hilda L. TA-CCCT Grant announcement. St. Petersburg College, Clearwater, Florida, September 19, 2012.

5. Meanness and Consequences

1. 24 Sauter, S. L. (2002). The changing organization of work and the safety and health of working people: Knowledge gaps and research directions. Cincinnati, OH: Dept. of Health and Human Services, Centers for Disease Control and Prevention, National Institute for Occupational Safety and Health.
2. Ibid.
3. Ibid.
4. Ibid.
5. 28 Lynch, J. J. (2000). A Cry Unheard New Insights Into the Medical Consequences of Loneliness. Baltimore, MD: Bancroft Press. Kindle Edition. 213 of 6839.
6. Ibid.
7. Blackwell, D.L., Lucas, J.W., Clark, T.C. National Health Interview Survey, 2012:Data From the National Health Interview Survey. Hyattsville, Md: U.S. Dept. of Health and Human Services, Centers for Disease Control and Prevention, National Center for Health Statistics.
8. Ibid.
9. Sternberg, E. M. (2000). The balance within: The science connecting health and emotions. New York: W.H. Freeman. Kindle location 366.
10. Health and Safety Executive. (2014). Stress and mental health at work. Retrieved from http://www.hse.gov.uk/stress/furtheradvice/stressandmentalhealth.htm
11. Azagba, Sunday and Sheraft, Mesbah F. Psychosocial working conditions and the utilization of health care services. BMC Public Health. August 11, 2011. Retrieved from http://www.biomedcentral.com/1471-2458/11/642

6. Learning From Two Very Different People

1. Jeannette Mcginnes died in 2022 after a life of incredible contribution and influence. She is enormously missed by those who knew and loved her.

7. Does Anybody Care?

1. Wilson, Ernest J. III. Empathy Is Still Lacking in the Leaders Who Need It Most. September 21, 2015.. Harvard Business Review. Retrieved from https://hbr.org/2015/09/empathy-is-still-lacking-in-the-leaders-who-need-it-most
2. UC Berkeley News. (2009).Some of us may be born more empathetic, new study suggests [Press Release]. Retrieved from http://www.berkeley.edu/news/media/releases/2009/11/16_empathy_gene.shtml

8. Communicating With Respect

1. Ludwig, Emil. Napoleon. (2014) Lulu Press. [Google Books]. Retrieved from https://books.google.com/books?id=u9lYCAAAQBAJ&dq=Only+the+strong+man+is+good%3B+the+weakling+is+evil+-+napoleon&source=gbs_navlinks_s
2. Lencioni, P. (2010). Getting Naked: A business fable about shedding the three fears that sabotage client loyalty. San Francisco, CA: Jossey-Bass. vii.
3. Economy, Peter. (2014). Seven Ways to End Every Meeting On a Positive Note. Inc.com. Retrieved from http://www.inc.com/peter-economy/7-effortless-ways-to-end-every-meeting-on-a-positive-note.html
4. Thompson, Derek. (2014). Happy Workers Richer Companies. The Atlantic. Retrieved from http://www.theatlantic.com/business/archive/2014/07/happy-workers-richer-companies/375151/
5. Semuels, Alana.(2014) A New Business Strategy: Treating Employees Well. The Atlantic. Retrieved from http://www.msn.com/en-us/money/smallbusiness/a-new-business-strategy-treating-employees-well/ar-BBfXgnw
6. Evans, Lisa. (2014). Should Office Culture Change to Accommodate Introverts?. Fast Company. Retrieved from http://www.fastcompany.com/3026196/leadership-now/should-office-culture-change-to-accommo date-introverts
7. Raghu, Krishnamoorthy.(2014). How GE Gives Leaders Time to Mentor and Reflect. Harvard Business Review. Retrieved from https://hbr.org/2014/03/how-ge-trains-its-future-leaders/
8. Greer, Lindred. Power Struggle? (2014). Why Your Top Performers Fight and What to Do About It. inc.com. Retrieved from http://www.inc.com/lindred-greer/leadership-minimize-conflicts-teams.html?cid=sf01001
9. Agence France-Presse. (2014). The CIA Has Suspended Its Iran Operations Chief Over His 'Abusive' Management Style. Business Insider. Retrieved from http://www.inc.com/lindred-greer/leadership-minimize-conflicts-teams.html?cid=sf01001

9. Filters, Scaffolds, Frames, and Uptalk

1. Richart, Amanda and Avaniti, Amalia. The use of high rise terminals in southern california english. (January 14, 2014). Acoustic Society of America. Proceedings of Meetings on Acoustics, vol 20, 060001
2. Williams, L.E., & Bargh, J.A. (2008). Experiencing physical warmth influences interpersonal warmth. Science, 322, 606-607.
3. Meier, Brian P., & Robinson, Michael D. (2004). Why the sunny side is up associations between affect and vertical position. Psychological Science. Vol. 15. Number 4. 243.
4. Lakoff, George. Don't Think of an Elephant!: Know Your Values and Frame the Debate: The Essential Guide for Progressives. White River Junction, VT: Chelsea Green Pub., 2004. 17
5. Riken Research. (2013). Largest neuronal network simulation achieved using K computer. [News Release]. Retrieved from http://www.riken.jp/en/pr/press/2013/20130802_1/

10. The Integrity of Proof

1. Devine, Dennis J., et al. Jury Decision Making: 45 Years of Empirical Research on Deliberating Groups. Psychology, Public Policy and Law 7.3 (2001): 622
2. Thompson, Elizabeth. personal communication, January 11, 2016.
3. Arendt, Hannah. (1978, 1977). The life of the mind. (Two volumes in one). Harcourt, Inc. New York. 10003.

11. Hear and Heal

1. Seuss, Dr.(1982). Horton Hears a Who! New York: Random House, 23.
2. Stavrositu, Carmen, Sundar, S. Shyam. Does Blogging Empower Women? Exploring the Role of Agency and Community. Journal of Computer-Mediated Communication 17 (2012) 369–386
3. UNICEF. (2002) Why Children Must Be Heard. [Press Release]. Retrieved from http://www.unicef.org/newsline/02pr67sowc.htm
4. Jones, David E. (2006). A Soldier's Story: The Power of Words. Bloomington, Indiana: Author House, 66.
5. Knight, S. (2009). NLP at Work: The essence of excellence. London: Nicholas Brealey.p.84.
6. Berger, W. (2014). A More Beautiful Question the Power of Inquiry to Spark Breakthrough Ideas. New York, NY: Bloomsbury.
7. Dee, Thomas S. and Sieversten. (2015) Hands Henrik. The Gift of Time? School Starting Age and Mental Health. (CEPA Working Paper No-1508). Stanford Center for Policy Analysis. Retrieved from http://cepa.stanford.edu/wp15-08

8. The Right Question Institute. The Right Question Strategy In Education and Beyond. 2015. Retrieved from http://rightquestion.org/about/strategy
9. The Right Question Institute. Experiencing the QFT. 2015. Retrieved from http://rightquestion.org/educators/resources/

12. Transparency

1. National Center on Birth Defects and Developmental Disabilities, Center for Disease Control. Infant Screening. March 3, 2015. Retrieved from http://www.cdc.gov/ncbddd/newbornscreening/index.html
2. Ziering, Amy (Producer), & Dick, Kirby. (Director). (2015). The Hunting Ground [Film]. United States: Chain Camera Pictures.
3. Peregrine, Michael W. "The 'Responsible Corporate Officer Doctrine' Survives to Perplex Corporate Boards." *Harvard Law School Forum on Corporate Governance,* 05 July 2017. Found at: https://corpgov.law.harvard.edu/2017/07/05/the-responsible-corporate-officer-doctrine-survives-to-perplex-corporate-boards/ in Jan, 2026.
4. 21 U.S.C. § 333(a)(1) (2015).
5. Martin, Ryan M., Boynton, Lois A. From liftoff to landing: NASA's crisis communications and resulting media coverage following the Challenger and Columbia tragedies. Public Relations Review 31 (2005) 253–261
6. Ziemer, Paul L. PhD. Assistant Secretary for Environmental Safety and Health United States Department of Energy. New Health and Safety Initiatives at the Department of Energy (DO). Speech to NASA Annual Occupational Health Program meeting. November 30, 1992. Retrieved from http://ntrs.nasa.gov/archive/nasa/casi.ntrs.nasa.gov/19940012136.pdf

13. Communicating Risks

1. Ibid
2. Jones, Bob Dorigo, Remove Child Before Folding: The 101 Stupidest, Silliest, and Wackiest Warning Labels Ever. Grand Central Publishing. February 28, 2009, p. 44.
3. Smith, Sam. "Chernobyl Report Surprisingly Detailed but Avoids Painful Truths, Experts Say." Washington Post, 26 August 1986.
4. Kahneman, Daniel and Tversky, Amos. "Prospect Theory: An Analysis of Decision under Risk." Econometrica, 1979, p. 263. https://doi.org/10.2307/1914185 - More in this can be found in several studies including: Chib V. S., Shimojo S., O'doherty J. P. (2014). The effects of incentive framing on performance decrements for large monetary outcomes: behavioral and neural mechanisms. J. Neurosci. 34, 14833–14844. 10.1523/jneurosci.1491-14.2014 [DOI] [PMC free article] [PubMed] Note that this text has appeared as an example in other writings by David

Day, including "Preventing Performance Choke a Handbook:Find Strength When You Are Out Front
5. National Research Council. *Improving Risk Communication.* National Academy Press. 1989, p.110.
6. Fischhoff, et al - editors. FDA p. 42.

14. Authenticity

1. Sears, William, MD, Sears, Martha, RN. 8 Ways To Raise An Expressive Child. Ask Dr Sears. 2015. Retrieved from http://www.askdrsears.com/topics/parenting/child-rearing-and-development/8-ways-raise-expressive-child

16. Persuasion to Change

1. The Formula for Change was developed by David Gleicher in the early 1960s and later revised by Kathie Dannemiller in the 1980s. Dannemiller simplified the Gleicher formula by changing the letters in the equation to coincide better with the wording of the description. Day has simplified the designations even further so the equation looks like what is included in this book.

17. Hitting a Moving Target

1. Reiner, Cedar. Willingham, Daniel. The Myth of Learning Styles. The Magazine of Higher Learning. August, 2010. 32-35.
2. Berne, E. (1964). Games People Play; The psychology of human relationships. New York; Grove Press

18. Choosing Language for a Growth Mindset

1. Dweck, Carol S. Mindset: The New Psychology of Success. New York: Random House, 2006.
2. Portions of the two preceding paragraphs appeared in an article on LinkedIn written by David L. Day, May 2, 2015.
3. Dweck, Carol, (2014) The power of believing you can improve. TED.-com. Retrieved from http://www.ted.com/talks/carol_dweck_the_power_of_believing_that_you_can_improve
4. Evans, Joseph. personal communication, January 11, 2016.

19. Pandemic and Politics

1. Maercker, Andreas and Horn, Andrea B. "A Socio-interpersonal Perspective on PTSD: The Case for Environments and Interpersonal Processes."

Clinical Psychology and Psychotherapy Clin. Psychol. Psychother. 2012. DOI: 10.1002/cpp.1805

20. A Most Dangerous World (and the power of humanity)

1. AIPRM. (2025). AI adoption statistics 2025/26. https://www.aiprm.com/ai-adoption-statistics/
2. (2025). A, Jordana "AI usage stats 2025." *Hostinger.* 28 November 2-25. https://www.hostinger.com/tutorials/how-many-companies-use-ai
3. Stanford HAI. (2025). "AI's influence on society has never been more pronounced." 2025 AI index report. Stanford University Human-Centered Artificial Intelligence. https://hai.stanford.edu/ai-index/2025-ai-index-report
4. AIPRM.
5. AIPRM
6. Microsoft. (2026). "Global AI Adoption in 2025 - A Widening Digital Divide" AI diffusion report, January 2026. https://www.microsoft.com/en-us/research/wp-content/uploads/2026/01/Microsoft-AI-Diffusion-Report-January-2026.pdf
7. Stanford
8. Kankar, Anit. "Spanning Radiology, Cardiology, Neurology and More, the List Highlights FDA's Ongoing Commitment to Advancing Safe and Effective AI Integration in Healthcare." *Med Tech Perspective,* 14 July 2025. https://www.medtechspectrum.com/analysis/12/24541/the-2025-index-100-fda-approved-ai-driven-medical-devices.html
9. Stanford HAI. (2025). "AI's influence on society has never been more pronounced." 2025 AI index report. Stanford University Human-Centered Artificial Intelligence. https://hai.stanford.edu/ai-index/2025-ai-index-report
10. Kennedy, Brian, Yam,Eilene, Kikuchi, Emma, Pula, Isabelle, Fuentes, Javier. "How Americans View AI and it's Impacts on People and Society." Pew Research Center. 17 September 2025. https://www.pewresearch.org/wp-content/uploads/sites/20/2025/09/PS_2025.9.15_AI-and-its-impact_report.pdf
11. Naik, Siddhi. "Global AI Statistics: Users, Market Size & Trends (2025)." Resourcera. Global AI statistics 2025. 28 November 2025 https://resourcera.com/data/artificial-intelligence/ai-statistics/

Acknowledgments

Thank you to Toby Johnson, PhD, my fearless and dedicated editor, who was extremely patient and helpful far beyond the call of duty in editing the original version of this book.

- Thank you also to Bobbie Evans, Liz Thompson, Jeannette McGinnis and Joey Evans, who graciously agreed to be included in examples in this book.

- I am grateful to my friend Bill Gardner, who inspired me by saying he was tired of seeing shallow, boring books about communication, and to my friend Carter Forringer, who encouraged me to find meaningful business examples.

- Special gratitude to Joel Hueske, who patiently heard almost everything in this book several times before it went on paper.

Some Graphics are AI-generated, but with significant editing by the author. Those are thus copyrighted in the version as presented herein.

About the Author

David Day – is an internationally known expert in business communication. For over thirty years he has conducted high-stakes communication coaching for executives of many of the largest companies in the world.

This work has included pharmaceutical, energy, utility, defense, nuclear, chemical and medical device companies. He has regularly prepared teams for crisis communication, regulatory hearings and issue resolution.

In over thirty years of consulting, Mr. Day has gained extensive knowledge of corporate business issues and communication approaches. Before his consulting career, he was President of a broadcast news network and Vice President of a corporation that owned a chain of broadcast stations. He is a member of the Society of Professional Journalists.

David holds a bachelor's degree from Saint Edward's University, where he majored in communication, and a Master of Arts Degree in Mass Communication from Texas State University. He is certified by *The Leadership Circle* for conducting executive and company culture profiles.

Also by David Day

Preventing Performance Choke - A Handbook: Find Strength When You Are Out Front

www.ingramcontent.com/pod-product-compliance
Lightning Source LLC
Chambersburg PA
CBHW031954190326
41520CB00007B/247

9780692654491